The "No Excuses" Mindset

A Life of Purpose, Passion, and Clarity

The "No Excuses" Mindset

A Life of Purpose, Passion, and Clarity

Farshad Asl

First Printing: 2016

Library of Congress Cataloging-in-Publication Data is available upon request.

Soft cover ISBN: 978-1-943526-71-0
Hard cover ISBN: 978-1-943526-72-7

Printed in the United States of America

Published by Author Academy Elite
P.O. Box 43, Powell, OH 43035
www.AuthorAcademyElite.com

Also available as an ebook and audiobook.

www.TopLeadersInc.com

Ordering Information: Special discounts are available on quantity purchases by corporations, associations, educators, and others. For details, contact www.Topleadersinc.com

Dedication

To my wife Mina
and my children Michelle and Rachelle.

To my father and mother who taught me
the "No Excuses" mindset.

To my wonderful readers;
your support is invaluable.

Contents

Acknowledgements

So many wonderful people have supported me through this journey in developing the clarity of the "No Excuses" mindset.

My mentor, **Dr. John C. Maxwell**, has taught me how to live a life of significance.

My incredible team at Bankers Life has given me the opportunity to serve them, learn from them, and grow with them.

My good friend Nathan Eckel, has inspired me to write this book by seeing the truth in me and by proclaiming that "Yes, I Can!" His faithfulness has always brought out the best in me.

My thinking partner and assistant, Malahat Zhobin, who has been of great support and encouragement to me.

Note to the Reader

A leader with great expectations develops a team of great performers. Mediocrity is not an option.

Every year, month, week, and even day people dream their dreams, set their goals, and make their plans. With high expectations they are hoped for but *rarely worked for*. Within our society, the majority of people don't meet expectations, this being around 80 percent, around 15 percent of people actually meet expectations, while about ***five percent of people exceed expectations***. These numbers derive from my own experience in the sales and management industry.

Now, the question arises, what sets apart the people who meet and exceed expectations from the rest of us? What do they do differently, what do they practice, how do they think? Below are 7 characteristics of people who exceed their own expectations.

1. **Clarity:**
   People who meet and exceed their expectations have a crystal clear picture of their mission at hand. Their clarity is composed of details and reasons. They focus on meaningful activities that bear results while having their sights set on their goal.

2. **Understanding the 10/90 Principle:**
   People who exceed their expectations understand that we do not have any control over 10 percent of

our lives. This is everything that happens to us while 90 percent of our lives are all about how we respond. They can turn a mediocre day into an exceptional day with the right course of *Action* and *Understanding*. We all start our days the same but end them differently based on the reactions we have toward the day's challenges and opportunities.

3. **Anticipation**:
   People who exceed expectations are **Active, not Reactive**; they are **Proactive, not Passive**. *Proactive Anticipation* makes the difference between a winner and a loser. They are **forward thinkers** who are intentional with their activities. They are always ready for what is to come by making adjustments before something happens. They are alert and prepared.

4. **Innovative:**
   Constant innovation. People who exceed expectations think outside the box; in fact, they don't even believe in a box. They are always finding new ways to do things, always getting ahead in the game, and are always setting and breaking records. They know where they want to go and how to construct their path to get there.

5. **Massive Action:**
   People who exceed expectations don't simply act; instead, they take massive action. This means that no matter what, they make it work! With full force and 120 percent energy, they are in it to win it. They give it their all and all they've got. They hustle, pay the price, and never give excuses. There are no simple gestures, only massive actions.

6. **Look your best:**

   Dress for success. People who exceed expectations not only act the part, they also look the part. Both inwardly and outwardly, they are at their best. They understand the significance and importance of first impressions. At every moment, they are ready.

7. **Compassion:**

   You've got to love what you do daily. No one has ever been able to succeed, let alone exceed, without compassion for what they do. People who exceed expectations are driven by their love for what they do. Their passion and purpose are aligned and meet triumphantly at the reality of their dreams and goals.

Now is the time to set your standards high and your expectations even higher. Be intentional with practicing and perfecting these champion characteristics. Don't become the excuse that is holding you back from your own success. Simply ask, what do you expect of yourself? Take advantage of this opportunity to inspire, encourage, and lead others by the examples you set for yourself. Let's start the "No Excuses" journey together.

Preface

Life is an uphill journey abundant with opportunities. This book is for the entrepreneur, the leader, the artist, the baby boomer, and the millennial. It is time to get a move on, to make the necessary strides to truly create a difference. In these pages, you will be introduced to an innovative decision-making process that will give you resources and access to alternatives. You will experience a paradigm shift and the true meaning of the 20/20 mindset.

In life, we all have found ourselves creating internally consistent justifications for our failures and shortcomings. This book will eliminate this by-product. When you learn to live without excuses you are empowered, equipped, and laser-focused to succeed.

So come along on this adventure to learn the skills and gain the characteristics that will eliminate the excuses from your life. Live the way you have always desired, to the fullest and complete ability by which God intended.

Introduction

This book presents a new way to overcome the challenges in your life. Fundamentally, it takes the very reasons we choose to remain dormant and turns them into our reasons to succeed. It does away with our natural tendency to accept failure and replaces it with powerful reasons to press on toward success. It eliminates all of our excuses from home, business or career—in fact, in every aspect of life.

The various sections of this book will illuminate the kinds of excuses that keep us from our goals, and will offer swift and compelling defenses against them. I'll share with you the means to an excuse-free mindset. You will be introduced to the 20/20 mindset, which is a new way of thinking that implores clarity and certainty in your vision, goals, and dreams.

With the 20/20 mindset you will be able to visualize, realize, and actualize your purpose and passion in life like never before. This mindset will eliminate any excuse and illuminate all possibilities. In the end, you will be liberated from fear and enthusiastically embrace a new form of living that will carry you to your goals.

When your **purpose** and **passion** are in alignment, your work becomes your calling, your life becomes your dream, and your **mindset** becomes **20/20** in clarity.

1. In Plain Sight

Four Hundred Dollars

It wasn't much, but it was all I had in my pocket. I was in the United States for a short time, and though I was in arguably the richest nation in the world, my fortune was a total of four hundred dollars.

Even with my unfamiliarity and lack of connections in a foreign land, I carried a hunger to succeed. My unrest was coupled with my hopes and dreams. I did not allow any hindrance or obstacle to become an excuse. I kept my dream alive.

I was sitting at the kitchen table flipping through the help wanted section of the newspaper. At the time, the Internet wasn't where you went to find work. It was the newspaper.

"Experience required." I had been here for more than a hundred days, but the kind of work I did in Iran—independent businessman, mushroom-farmer—didn't translate well into measurable experience.

"Strong command of the English language is a must." I could carry on a casual conversation and could ask enough questions to help me find my way.

With my unrest and eagerness to get my life started in America, combined with the never-ending challenges I faced, I could have easily surrendered to living a life full of excuses.

This is a tough market. Nobody is hiring. The economy is not good. I don't know the language. I don't have money. I don't have any connections, etc.

But the reasons I came to this country had more to do with the opportunities, freedom of choice, my faith, and my family. These things were far more valuable than any excuse I could give. I knew exactly **why** I chose to be here.

Then I came across an advertisement for insurance sales. I asked my wife, Mina, her thoughts. I knew she always had good ideas, and wondered about her opinion on this matter.

"Well," she said, "if it goes well then great. I think you will add value to many lives with this opportunity since it is aligned with your purpose and passion to help people."

My Mina is a woman of great perspective, wisdom, unconditional love, and support.

Making the Calls

The insurance job that was being offered was by Bankers Life. The job sounded pretty good, but the details were a bit unclear to me. When I went for the interview, I was afraid my thick accent would stand in the way.

At any rate, I learned the job was fundamentally all about prospecting and marketing yourself. Since I didn't know anyone, my last resort was direct call phone sales.

"Hello, My Name is Farshad, and..."

Click.

Each time my heart got a bit heavier, but I knew the truth. The only way to get an appointment was to make the call.

By the end of the third day of calling, I was nearing *three hundred consecutive calls* per day without as much as a full conversation. I decided there might be something wrong with the script for it to have failed so many times.

Again, Mina offered to help. As I began reciting the script for her, I was completely surprised by her assessment.

"Hello, ma'am," I began. "My name is Farshad..."

"Well, my love, I think I know your problem."

As she interrupted at about the same time every caller had hung up on me, I thought she might be onto something.

"What is it, Mina? What am I doing wrong?"

"I think the problem might not be with the script, but with your name."

Change my name? I grew uncomfortable with the idea.

What Mina was noting was a possibility I had never in my life considered, and though it might seem clever and innovative, the suggestion was a galvanizing moment in my life.

Had I chosen at that moment, for instance, to become Farshad "Fred" Asl, I might have begun to have immediate success setting appointments.

"Fred" is of course a far more 'acceptable' name. But my intentions were to build a successful brand with my name Farshad, not Fred.

> But my intentions were to build a successful brand with my name Farshad, not Fred.

In that moment, life became a bit clearer for me. I was going to keep making calls and I was going to get appointments. I didn't directly know HOW but I had found more clarity with WHY.

The very next day as I began to make the calls, I concentrated on the purpose of my calling, not just on the words of the script. I worked on my diction so my name would be easier to understand.

"Hello, I'm FARSHAD ASL..."

Click!

"Hello, I'm FARSHAD ASL. I would like to..."

Click!

"Hello, I'm FARSHAD ASL... I would like to talk to you about..."

Click!

Then, after more than three hundred consecutive calls, I finally got through that introductory script unhindered. There was silence on the other end of the line and I feared I might have just missed the 'click!' Then, miracle of miracles, the woman with whom I was speaking spoke up.

"Young man, I have absolutely no idea what you are talking about; I couldn't understand what you were saying. But if you want, I suppose we can set a time for you to come see me, so you can explain yourself face to face."

I'd gotten my first appointment. The bar had been exceeded, and the rule of numbers was once again validated. It isn't the number of calls one makes that matters; it is that they make the call.

The Lesson of the Brochure

Now that I had my first appointment, the next challenge on my plate was doing a full presentation. As I drove out to the appointment, I was nervous and very excited at the same time.

The woman, in her early seventies, was pleasant and warm, and was actually quite pleased that I had come. High with emotions of excitement, I gave her a hug. When we got past the small talk, I explained my challenge with English, and asked her, "Can we read the brochure together?"

With a warm smile, she said, "Okay, let's go for it."

As we read the brochure together and discussed its contents, we marked right on the paper the parts that struck her personally as the important pieces of the insurance program. I gained as much as she did out of the presentation.

My experience with this woman eradicated any excuse I could ever give. I had no reason to give excuses. I knew what

I was capable of achieving. She gave me the **hope** that I needed.

After breaking the ice with her, I went on to make many more sales. She was my first; what I gained from that first encounter set my feet upon the path that I follow to this day. She has positively impacted my life and career. The value she added to my life still resonates today where I find myself overseeing over 20 different offices. All I needed was that defining moment.

The Trouble with the Car

Now, a salesman, particularly one who deals in insurance, has to maintain a certain image of being respectable and trustworthy in order to avoid any negative feelings about the actual transactions.

We had only one car at the time. Now, to be fair, I had gotten a pretty good deal on it and it worked just fine. But in all honesty, it was a wreck, literally. While the driver's side looked pristine—no dings, no dents, no weird punctures, or rust—the passenger's side gave the car its personality. The vehicle had been in a considerable accident, leaving the passenger's side obliterated. Still, I needed a car to get to my appointments.

In time, I mastered the charade of this car. I knew exactly where and how to park and position the car in order to present its good side. This practice taught me to value what did have, even if it was half a car. I would use what I had to make the best impressions without any excuses. In my case, I was literally presenting the best side of my car to aid me with my first impression. Your first impression will set the foundation of any relationship you will build, including your clientele. Today, this story is well known as "Farshad's half a car story."

The Rest of the Car... Story

As soon as I earned some extra money, I considered looking for either a really good deal on parts or an incredibly good deal on another car.

I went to the junkyard in search of a new body for my half a car. Luckily, I found what I was looking for, the exact body my car needed. When I asked the owner what he would charge for the wreck he quoted one thousand dollars, almost double what I could afford.

Immediately, without hesitation I offered him half of what he asked. Stunned by the low offer, instead of negotiating, he asked, "How can you only offer me half of what I was asking?"

I answered honestly. "I only want to buy half the car, that's all I need. I already have the other half."

> "I only want to buy half the car, that's all I need. I already have the other half."

The humor and honesty of my offer convinced the man to sell me the whole body for "half the car" price.

I still had so much to learn. You see, I might have never gotten the deal if I hadn't been able to have fun with the negotiation and told the truth.

If you hold in your mind a clear intent and ask exactly what you want, if the timing and opportunity are right, you will receive what you ask for.

Getting the Performance You Deserve

"Whatever is true, whatever is noble, whatever is right, whatever is pure, whatever is lovely, whatever is admirable—if anything is excellent or praiseworthy— think about such things."

—Philippians 4:8-9

What we put into our minds is what we get out. It is common knowledge that a computer cannot output something it was not programmed to do. In early years, computer science programmers developed the phrase "garbage in, garbage out" (GIGO), meaning that if you program bad code into a computer your results will be faulty.

Our minds also work according to the GIGO principle. The kinds of things we watch, read, listen to, and think about will affect the way we talk, feel, and live. One of my favorite stories is in Matthew 13:

A farmer went out to plant some seeds. As he scattered them across his field, some seeds fell on a footpath, and the birds came and ate them. Other seeds fell on shallow soil with underlying rock. The seeds sprouted quickly because the soil was shallow. But the plants soon wilted under the hot sun, and since they didn't have deep roots, they died. Other seeds fell among thorns that grew up and choked out the tender plants. Still other seeds fell on fertile soil, and they produced a crop that was thirty, sixty, and even a hundred times as much as had been planted.

Our thought patterns are like a piece of land. What kind of mindset would you choose to have? What percentage of your mind is actively producing results? What's your mental diet like? What kind of thoughts do you have? Are they nutritious thoughts that taste good to your mind and heart? Or are they junk food thoughts that steal your physical and emotional energy, your hope, your happiness, and your enthusiasm?

As a metaphor, rational thought and reasoned consideration is needed for a healthy diet for the mind. When we allow ourselves to ignore a rational option in favor of an irrational one, or perhaps an unjustified one, it's like eating junk food. It fills the need for making a decision but does so with no decision at all. Just like junk food, it satiates the need to act, but it requires no action at all.

Just as a fast burst of junk food can enliven your body, then let it down soon after, so can an excuse fulfill the need for rational decision only for a little while. In the case of an accepted excuse, guilt results. Your course toward success suffers.

It's time to eliminate excuses from your mental diet. This is the "No Excuses" mindset.

As Romans 12:2 says,

> "Do not conform to the patterns of this world, but be transformed by the renewing of your mind."

A "No Excuses" mindset focuses on what we **can** do. A "No Excuses" mindset focuses on **why** we desire to succeed, and then derives the means to achieve it. James Allen, in his book *As a Man Thinketh*, said:

> A man's mind may be likened to a garden, which may be intelligently cultivated or allowed to run wild; but whether cultivated or neglected, it must, and will, bring forth. If no useful seeds are put into it, then an abundance of useless weed seeds will fall therein, and will continue to produce their kind.

It seems like a minor detail, but what we focus on makes all the difference. Choosing to focus on the tiny thing that is positive will make the difference between success and failure. Focusing on the right things is a key component for success. The "No Excuses" mindset focuses on what is improving and what is valuable.

The "No Excuses" mindset is just that: no excuses. To do this, you must have clarity in your thinking, and there is a secret weapon I use to get clarity. If you are serious about learning to live without excuses, you will want this secret too! In fact, this is the very heart of the "No-Excuses" mindset. It is called the "3D Mental Process."

The 3D Mental Process

At a glance, the "3D Mental Process" is made up of:

- Crystal Clear Visions
- Strategic Plans
- Measurable Outcomes

1. Crystal Clear Vision

Recall a time when you were traveling with your parents as a youngster. It was a fun, joyful, and even peaceful experience. Even though you didn't know the direction, destination, or purpose, you were so excited just to be with your parents. The journey was clear and straightforward; even bumpy roads didn't bother you because you were with them.

You trusted them and found peace in their *crystal clear vision*. The only important question for you was, "Are we there yet? Are we there yet?" You believed in their vision, and therefore, were able to enjoy the journey without any concerns.

Now let's imagine you were with your parents and they didn't know where they were going. No direction, no destination, no certainty, resulting in an unpleasant journey. Your mind would worry. It would not be peaceful. Without clarity, the dynamic of this trip becomes completely different. The power of a crystal clear vision is huge...it's amazing.

People with clear vision complain less, worry less, and instead are focused on achieving their end result. This clarity becomes the fuel for reaching the goal. A clear vision gives you the positive energy to start taking massive action, and in return, that massive action gives you even more energy to continue. That is how you will lead your life with purpose, passion, and a clear mind.

Life is a moving target. So your *vision* needs to be an accurate objective, to give you direction for your actions. As you move toward your goal, the vision becomes even more substantive, more palpable. It becomes something you can't wait to share with others continually. The excitement is infectious.

Sharing such a clear, concise vision spawns a sense of purpose and direction. It attracts success toward you and helps you build an expanding team. Success naturally follows from a strong central vision.

Every day, there are countless examples of ordinary and humble people who tenaciously achieve their goals. They are the ones who keep the wheels turning in any organization. Let's start with just one. He was originally called Saul of Tarsus, but later became better known as Saint Paul. In 2 Corinthians 4:16 and 18, he wrote:

> Every day, there are countless examples of ordinary and humble people who tenaciously achieve their goals.

"Therefore we do not lose heart...We fix our eyes not on what is seen, but on what is unseen. For what is seen is temporary, but what is unseen is eternal."

Paul's outlook allowed him to undergo intense hardship and pain with an unwavering faith in God. For him, it wasn't as much a matter of will and determination as it was a matter of vision and perspective.

My Vision Board
To remain focused on my goal, I created a 'vision board.' If you are unfamiliar with this, a vision board is a physical space for you to put images and inspirational messages as a tangible means to feed those mentally nutritional messages into your life, helping to accomplish your goal. It is a way that you can put eyes on the target visually and remind yourself constantly of what it takes to achieve it.

Many use vision boards with objectives that focus on getting a dream car, home, vacation, or maybe some form of monetary gain. My own vision board was like that until I received coaching and identified that the objectives had changed.

It shifted from where I once measured success by my possessions; I now measured it by comparing *who I was* with *who I want to become.* My vision board went from being **transitional to transformational,** from being about **success to significance.**

Now, my vision board captures the person I want to be, the virtues I want to manifest, and the kind of gentleness and genuine care I want to express. The focus has gone from me to others.

So, when you recognize your own core objectives, why not take your vision to a whole new level? Review your perspective and challenge yourself to project your vision board three, five, or ten years from now about the person you want to become, not just the material things you want to possess. You'll experience an incredible shift in your outlook.

> "Your visions will become clear only when you can look into your own heart. Who looks outside, dreams; who looks inside, awakes."
>
> —C.G. Jung

2. Strategic Planning

What you do daily and what you find in your daily agenda turn into your habits. Your habits guide and sculpt your path. The same process that builds habits can break habits. Nevertheless, it will take intentionality and consistency to replace your old habits and routines with new ones that will get you closer to your vision in life. Align your activity with your vision. Being consistent and intentional with your daily activities will result in sustainable success.

Making the transition from the old to the new is difficult and uncomfortable. Nevertheless, if you focus on the "why" you will be guided to the "how." It is in our nature to overcome any challenge we are faced with. Our defense mechanisms intend to protect us from discomfort and challenges, but our willpower is limitless and can face and defeat those challenges.

This process of breaking the old habits and making new ones requires strategic planning. Your vision is your *why*, while your strategic plan is your *how*. Even though the details are essential and knowing your numbers are important, it is the burning desire in your heart that will get you to the outcome you expect.

> "May he give you the desire of your heart and make all your plans succeed."
>
> —Psalm 20:4

Let's take a look at a great example from the book of Exodus. Moses wasn't much of a strategic thinker until God commanded him to become one. In fact, Moses began by creating excuses, telling the Almighty God that he had no skills in such things and that he was a poor public speaker.

Though Moses struggled as a leader even after he led the nation of Israel out of Egypt, his *why* rose above any excuse he could give. With strategic planning and help from his father-in-law, Jethro, he was able to delegate the work so that the load would be spread among many. As a result, the manpower resources were used more effectively and the ministry was accomplished.

While the early passages demonstrate his initial ineptitude, Moses was clearly thinking strategically by the time he sent spies to the land of Canaan. His passion and purpose were aligned with his vision, and with guidance from the Lord, success became a reality. Vision leads to proper planning, and proper planning leads to successful completion.

Execution is key; how you follow through with your plan is crucial. There is a big difference between motion and action. Just because you get out of bed doesn't mean you are making progress. Taking action requires decisiveness, dedication, and a clear direction.

If you have chosen to accept no excuses, then the execution becomes second nature. You planned it, so you will accomplish it. We call this *commitment*. Let me make this clear, the definition of being committed is getting things done with absolutely no excuse, with an unshakeable and undeniable passion and with an uncompromised integrity.

Always know that you are being held accountable for your actions, by your friends, family, coworkers, and most importantly, by God. Lead by example and build a team of successful people around you. By being the dependable person, success is naturally attracted to you.

When it comes to strategic planning, the most common question raised is how to effectively manage time. I have news for you. You can't manage time. You can only manage your life. You can't strategically plan time, you can only plan your life.

Know what you want to accomplish in life, identify your purpose, and align it with your passion. When you are crystal clear on this matter and are laser-focused on your end goals, your time will be "managed" as effectively as your life. A purpose-driven life is a well-managed life. Successful life management and planning is about fine-tuning your TO DO and NOT TO DO lists. Everything in life will fall into one of the following categories:

- **Do it now.**
  There are things in life that require a sense of urgency; don't put them off. Take action and just do it now.

- **Do it through others.**
  Delegate. True leaders understand the importance of delegation—they know that they can't do everything on their own. We must accept the fact that we can't be good at everything.

- **Do it later.**
  Procrastinate with purpose. Intentionally set time aside to get minor tasks, projects, and responsibilities done. Box them away for a later time and date. Don't let the minor things in life influence your effectiveness today while you focus on the major things in life.

- **Don't do it at all.**
  Change your habits. Identify areas in your life that occupy your time but don't bear any fruit. If it's not adding any value to you or others, and if it's not getting you closer to your purpose, then don't do it at all.

- **Do it with enthusiasm.**
  Do it with passion or don't do it at all. Nothing significant has ever been accomplished without enthusiasm. Give it all you got, stay consistent, and never give up.

Life management is not about BUSYNESS; it is about PRODUCTIVENESS and EFFECTIVENESS—major on the major things in life, not on minors. Think about your future and work towards it now. Forward thinkers create a plan, focus on the plan, and execute the plan. Procrastinators just talk about the plan, get distracted with minor things, and postpone the plan. We don't need time management; we need life management with purpose.

> Forward thinkers create a plan, focus on the plan, and execute the plan.

"You have to have confidence in your ability and then be tough enough to follow through."

—Rosalynn Carter

3. Measurable Outcomes

> "Train a child in the way he should go: and when he is
> old, he will not depart from it."
>
> —Proverbs 22:6

Every plan has an outcome. But the outcome is bifold; there are two sides to it. Most people only ever consider to think about the positive outcome in achieving a goal. Seldom do people consider the outcome of not achieving their desired results. This balance is essential to maintain. It is the key to the 3D Mental Process.

Directly experiencing the positive end result of our goals is a powerful incentive to pursue a vision and enact a plan. Nevertheless, consequences also offer a valuable and refining incentive that can be equally powerful when properly experienced.

So what motivates you more? The fear of failure or the fantastic feeling of achieving your dreams? It's important to recognize how an outcome influences you, and how to best configure your responses in order to motivate yourself. Self-accountability means understanding these concepts:

- The positive consequences that come with achieving the goal.
- The negative consequences that come with not achieving the goal.

Putting the 3D Mental Process into Action

If you desire to experience the 3D Mental Process, you must understand that it is a trifold process. You need a clear vision, a strategic plan, and a measurable outcome. With the 3D Mental Process you will meet expectations, but in order to exceed expectations, there is one more important factor that needs to be explored. What makes the difference between a person who meets his expectations and a person who exceeds them is his **mindset**.

What you need is a 20/20 mindset. This is a mindset of complete clarity and no self-doubt. Mindsets matter. A great example is Michael Jordan. Let's take a peek into his 20/20 mindset:

- "Some people want it to happen, some wish it would happen, and others make it happen."
- "Obstacles don't have to stop you. If you run into a wall, don't turn around and give up. Figure out how to climb it, go through it, or work around it."
- "If you quit ONCE it becomes a habit. Never quit!!!"
- "I've missed more than 9,000 shots in my career. I've lost almost 300 games. 26 times, I've been trusted to take the game winning shot and missed. I've failed over and over and over again in my life. And that is why I succeed."
- "You must expect great things of yourself before you can do them."

A 20/20 mindset produces clarity, joy, and peace in your life. It produces RESULTS. When your purpose and passion are in alignment, your work becomes your calling, your life becomes your dream, and your mindset becomes 20/20 in clarity. You begin to live to your full potential.

When your vision is clear for your life, goals, and dreams, the confidence and assurance gained bear fruit to joy and peace. A 20/20 mindset eradicates any source of fear, doubt, and uncertainty. It produces a balanced life in which you are living your purpose and being fueled with your passion. You are connected directly to the source of greatness. Success is then a graceful gift.

When you live with a 20/20 mindset your path is straight, vision is clear, and decisions are precise. You see the bigger picture with a broader view and incorporate different angles and perspectives. You optimize your vision's capabilities and peripherals, whether you are at 20/20, near-sighted, or far-sighted.

Your decisions are calculated and intentional, leaving no room for any excuses. You walk by faith and not by sight, because you do not hope for your future; instead, you envision it with detail, clarity, and confidence. Your expectations for what is to come and for other people are built on solid foundations, creating higher standards and greater value in your life, relationships, family, and friends.

A 20/20 mindset produces uncontainable joy and peace. These fruits allow you to live more creatively, effectively, and positively. When your life is in alignment with your purpose

> Nothing will hold you back because you expect the unexpected.

and your passion, then working hard and creating value are inherent and success becomes a given.

With a 20/20 mindset, there is constant growth in both your personal and professional life. Nothing will hold you back because you expect the unexpected. With a clear vision for your life, you are better prepared to combat any opposition.

With determination and focus, a life that employs a 20/20 mindset makes a deep impact, its own imprint in the world and in the lives of others.

Challenge yourself to live with a 20/20 mindset. You too will think, see, act, and live with clarity like never before. You will be able to visualize, realize, and actualize your passion and purpose, and bring them to alignment.

Interact

In the blanks allotted below, feel free to answer the questions as succinctly, or as openly, as you choose. This will provide you a solid baseline for your success in the future, and a barometer of your current confidence level in your own success potential.

Vision: Do I have a vision for what I want to do?

Plan: What is my plan for accomplishing my vision?

Outcome: How can I anticipate both positive and negative outcomes, and how can I learn to grow from them?

20/20 Mindset: On a scale of 1-5, score your

- Clarity of Mind   1 2 3 4 5
- Clarity of Vision   1 2 3 4 5
- Clarity of Plan   1 2 3 4 5

2. Renovating the Mind

Four Steps to a Paradigm Shift

- Challenge your paradigm
- Ask questions
- Be open to change
- Take decisive action

> "You can't change the fruit without changing the root."
>
> —Stephen R. Covey

An old saying states that a journey of a thousand miles begins with a single step. So, at what point do we embark on this adventure? How do we begin this journey toward a "No Excuses" life? Below are 4 important steps that will shake your foundation, break up your routines, and unblock your current mindset.

Doing so will open your eyes and more readily allow you to utilize the 3D thinking and the 20/20 mindset to their fullest extent. So let's begin this journey; let's take it one step at a time, and you will soon find yourself with no room for excuses and every reason to expect greater success.

STEP 1: Challenge Your Paradigm

"We don't see things as they are, we see things as we are."

—Anais Nin

Everyone has a paradigm, a "lens" through which they view the world around them. This paradigm impacts the way we observe and interpret what we see. Most don't think about or take into account what sorts of things influence their perception of the world. They simply accept what they see, as if it is static, immovable, and unchanging. Even fewer know how to retrain their minds or alter their paradigm. For them, such change would be unimaginable to accomplish.

The inquisitive nature of youth should carry over into our adult lives. Challenging the status quo and enticing curiosity should be a daily practice of adult life. We must reinvigorate that incessant drive in order to adopt a "No Excuses" mindset. It isn't a new revelation, but rather, a radical change in what we know about ourselves—our minds, our souls, our wills, and our emotions. It is a massive reconditioning, a complete reboot of the fundamental shift in how we view reality.

> Challenging the status quo and enticing curiosity should be a daily pratice of adult life.

Our culture bombards us with the false notion that success is to have "things." We dream about having the right car, the right house, the right position, and the right image. I know how that mindset feels; for decades, I felt the same way but I have found that success can be and should be measured differently. Success is not about what you have; instead, it's about who you are becoming.

After my paradigm shifted, a transformation took place within me and my dream of success no longer looked the same. I replaced the picture of my dream boat, dream house, dream job with a mirror! It wasn't about my possessions any longer, but rather, my **spirit**. I was no longer focused on what I had but on what I could be as a person, a husband, and a father.

What this concept means for you is monumental. Getting your eyes off what you have and onto who you really are is very important. The triangle of success for a person with the "No Excuses" mindset is not only composed of **net worth**, but also **self worth** and **network**. This paradigm shift will help you go from success to significance.

STEP 2: Ask Questions

> "Philosophers are adults who persist in asking childish questions."
>
> —Isaiah Berlin

As children, it is permissible, and in fact expected that we ask questions. We usually ask a lot of questions from those whom we trust will give us good answers.

"Why is the sky blue?"

"What is air made of?"

"What is night?"

"Why is the ocean salty?"

"How long do my fingernails grow in a month?

"How many hairs do I have?"

It is this innate curiosity that makes childhood so special, and it creates the needed space for the rapid expansion of knowledge we experience growing up. Ironically, when we believe that we have learned the answers, we often close other avenues of discovery. In essence, we train ourselves to STOP being inquisitive.

Why is that?

There are as many answers to this question as there are philosophers. It is argued by some that knowledge is power. From that standpoint they suggest that the reverse is also true, that a lack of knowledge exemplifies a lack of power. So, in order not to appear weak, we act as if we know it all. The reality is that we never really stop learning, though we might choose to no longer seek knowledge directly.

There is a vulnerability that we exhibit when we choose to continue learning. As most would acknowledge, the best way to learn and grow is to ask questions. Asking questions opens us up to new ideas and perspectives. They transform our thinking and draw out solutions. It produces a mindset that, by nature, has to be receptive to new information. That openness brings forth the realization that we may not know everything.

"There are none so blind as they who will not see."

—Thomas Heywood, 1546

So the second step, after developing a new paradigm, is to learn to ask the right questions and allow an inquisitive spirit to reawaken. To have no excuses means one must ask questions. You only get answers to the questions you ask, and even better, your answers may lie in the questions you ask. The time you spend with people becomes valuable through the type of questions you ask of them.

Asking questions opens up new doors, new opportunities, and new ideas. It helps you think, create, and discover. A great book to reference in this matter is *Good Leaders Ask Great Questions* by John C. Maxwell. Now, ask yourself, do any excuses remain?

"Others have seen what is and asked, 'Why?' I have seen what could be and asked, 'Why not?'"

—Pablo Picasso

STEP 3: Be Open To Change

"There are four important questions in life, 'Why? Why not? Why not me? Why not now?'"

—James Allen

Change is a difficult process. It can truly take place in an environment of support, structure, and sacrifice. Support comes from asking for help, seeking professional coaching, and surrounding yourself with the right people. Structure requires accountability, a follow-up system, and action. Sacrifice requires paying the price, getting out of your comfort zone but staying in your strength-zone.

> "And be not conformed to this world: but be transformed by the renewing of your mind, that ye may prove what is that good and acceptable, and perfect will of God."
>
> —Romans 12:2

STEP 4: Take Decisive Action

> "Change your thoughts and you change your world."
>
> —Norman Vincent Peale

Decisiveness is the number one quality of a dynamic leader; his ability to communicate a decision with passion and integrity is an art form.

> *Decisiveness is the number one quality of a dynamic leader.*

Too often, decisiveness is overlooked. Nevertheless, it is one of the most important characteristics of the "No Excuses" mindset that results in a successful paradigm shift. Indecisiveness is the number one reason for failure. When we can't make the right decisions, we start blaming, procrastinating, and giving excuses. So stop hoping that someday things will change, and start focusing your energy on the "why" instead of just the "how." When you find your *why* you will find your way, and from this point on, your level of commitment will help you finish the project in hand.

I would like to offer a new definition for commitment:

Commitment is not *just trying*, being interested, or promising that it will be done someday, sometime, or somewhere. The true definition of being committed is *getting things done* with absolutely **no excuses**, with an unshakeable and undeniable **passion,** and an uncompromising **integrity.**

Growing up, I always observed how my parents responded to the challenges that they faced. It was rare to witness them giving excuses or giving up. Life wasn't always easy, but there were principles in my parents' lives that exhibited the conditions that I now call "No Excuses." As kids, we didn't face the same hardships as our parents did, because these challenges were always met head on by our parents. Our parents modeled the life of "No Excuses" by seeing the challenges and choosing a course to correct or overcome them.

When my father's work was no longer viable, he made a change—he became an entrepreneur and started all over again. While his friends and colleagues were resistant to making changes, my father acted. From him I learned adaptability, innovation, and tenacity. In the same fashion, as I began to face challenges in my life, I followed his examples, learned the same concepts, and carried them forward in my life with the perspective I gained from him.

What is essential to know is that it is up to you to take action—sometimes, massive action. In order to change the things that are in your control, you must discover in yourself the skills, attributes, and characteristics necessary for a "No Excuses" lifestyle.

In an educational study titled "Introduction to Peterism," (Curtis & Anthony), people were given a **new concept** (such as the earth is round, or that eschatology is tied to soteriology) and were asked to believe it. This meant they would be required to set aside some of the things they already believed in, or a paradigm shift. This is very applicable to understanding the concept of a paradigm shift.

50 percent of the people believed it immediately—without thinking.

30 percent didn't believe it, immediately—without thinking.

15 percent wanted to wait until they made up their minds, but asked for no clarification and no further information.

5 percent analyzed all the details and finally came to a conclusion.

The results of the study show that an estimated **5 percent of people think**, 15 percent of people think they think, and 80 percent of people would rather die than think. When I first learned about these percentages, it awakened a restlessness and a sense of urgency in my stream of consciousness that I soon realized might lie dormant in the majority of people today.

How often do we think using intentional thinking versus obligatory thinking? At that, what percentage of our jobs and lives require intentional thinking? With the current trajectory of technology's relationship with our lives, soon enough all the thinking will be done for us. We live in an era of *smart* everything: smart phone, smart watch, smart home, and smart car. Now where does that leave us...*smart us*? If all the thinking is being done for us, as a byproduct, reflection becomes obsolete too. What happens to our perspectives and paradigm shifts?

Reflection is an all-consuming, in-depth, and serious thought process that is required in a paradigm shift. Here lie the plains for consideration, contemplation, deliberation, meditation, rumination, and pondering—the quintessence of the 3D Mindset. This is the key to success in any and all realms of your life, even your mindset, the 20/20 mindset.

American businessman, entrepreneur, investor, and philanthropist, Warren Buffett, is the most successful investor in the world. The secret to his success is that he spends 80 percent of every day reading. During this time, he is thinking and reflecting on what he is learning. He then plans his success based on the knowledge he has gained, which through practice becomes his insight. Through the reflection process, any level of success through a paradigm shift can become attainable. Here is how...

- **Reflection allows you to learn from your mistakes and failures.** It is a great habit to reflect on past experiences, whether they were bad or good; they are the stepping stones toward your success. Learning from your past will ensure you keep yourself from repeating it. In order to move forward, you must be able to reflect on your past. If you know where you are coming from, then you will know where you are going. Remove yourself from distractions. Set aside time for reflection—it is important to find a time to do your thinking. When planning your day, week, or activity, add a step and leave some time for reflection after the project is completed.

- **Reflection gives you a sense of satisfaction and accomplishment.** Through the course of reflection, you will gain joy, confidence, and a sense of fulfillment. Understanding and accepting the decisions you have made, good or bad, will make you bolder. Reflection helps punctuate your past and indent your future.

- **Reflection provides you with the best lessons.** As you practice reflecting on your past, you are equipped with the most powerful stories, lessons, and experiences to share. People tend to pay more attention to you when you are sharing something personal and meaningful to them. This is when you are able to connect with them on a personal level; I like to call this *leveling yourself with people*. Here is where you are adding value to people and are having the biggest and most realistic impact.

- **Reflection makes you think and think more often.** As mentioned before, reflection is an in-depth and serious thought process. You are required to think and think deeply. Practicing reflection pulls you out of your comfort zone and out of the autopilot society we live in. It breaks any routine and ignites a fire in your stream of consciousness. Practicing reflection daily ensures a healthy and invigorating lifestyle for both your mind and body. Your thoughts will be the key to your success.

- **Reflection turns your knowledge into insight.**
  There is a difference between knowledge and insight.
  We all know plenty of things, but what do we do with
  what we know? In our current society, we would
  rather *Google* or *YouTube* how to do something rather
  than think it through. We have become too lazy and
  too busy to think. It is crucial to understand the
  difference between knowledge, which are facts and
  data; wisdom, which is your ability to judge and
  determine which aspects of your knowledge are
  applicable and useful to your life; and insight, which
  is the deepest level of knowing based on experience,
  and the most meaningful to your life and success.
  When knowledge is put
  into practice then
  through your experience
  of it, it becomes your
  insight. Your insight is
  your asset; the edge you
  require to succeed.

> When knowledge is
> put into practice then
> through your experi-
> ence of it, it becomes
> your insight.

Success is a personal matter and its variables depend on you.
It is contingent to how often you think and reflect, how you
implore your insight and explore a paradigm shift. I used to
practice a culminating act of reflection at the end of every
year by looking back on everything that happened that year
and highlighting my greatest accomplishments and failures. I
would then share it with my family, friends, and colleagues.

This was when my knowledge became insight, and I added
value to both my life and others'. This was when and where
new perspectives were discovered. Although this was a good
habit and practice, I found that it wasn't enough. If I want

to be successful and reach the greatest heights, then I must become intentional about reflection.

If my insight will be the cause and determining factor of my success, then intentionally developing it through reflection will be my **daily practice**. What will you gain from reflection, because there is nothing to lose? Give yourself 30 minutes a day to think, reflect, and connect to gain new perspectives. You will be able to experience the edge required for success.

Interact

In the blanks allotted, answer the questions as succinctly, or as openly, as you choose. This will provide you necessary feedback on your progress.

Vision: Am I allowing an old paradigm to cloud my vision? Do I ask questions and open my mind to new ways of thinking?

Plan: Am I resistant to change? How can I plan to change for the better?

Outcome: What would happen if I employed the 4 steps outlined in this chapter? How different will my life look in 1, 3, and 5 years?

3. Coaching

Teacher, Mentor, Coach - what's the big deal?

> "Coaching closes the gap between thinking about doing and doing."
>
> —Curly Martin

The terms and concepts of Teacher, Mentor, and Coach can be challenging to decipher. For a long time I wondered, "What is the real difference between a coach, a mentor, and a teacher?" Not only was I unsure about the differences, but I also didn't have anyone who could consistently lead me in the right direction.

As I grew up and began to understand the importance of having a coach, mentor, or teacher, I still didn't grasp the differences. Only after doing some research and attending a few seminars did I learn the importance and distinction of each of these three roles in our lives.

Teachers

> "One child, one teacher, one book, one pen can change the world."
>
> —Malala Yousafzai

When it comes to learning, just about everyone can understand the meaning of "Teacher." Teachers instruct using a textbook or reference materials to provide lessons. This is a very important role to have in your life while you're growing up and when you're learning a subject or profession. Teachers have a talent for expressing information in a way we can accept and learn from.

Teachers build foundations, inspire core values, and create templates that structure our paradigms. Teaching is primarily about transmission of information: a teacher will pass knowledge onto his or her students for the purpose of self-improvement and preparation for life.

Mentors

Mentors share their wisdom and experience. They are willing to spend their time and expertise to guide the development of another person. They have walked the path and can tell you about their successes and failures. They can give you lessons, share best practices, and even demonstrate these through their actions.

Furthermore, they offer context—sharing why things are done the way they are, and demonstrating the value of particular education. In essence, they are the connective tissue of personal development. Mentors show you the *how*. They teach you from life experiences and equip you with valuable lessons.

Coaches

While a teacher will give you information and a mentor will share their experience, a coach will primarily do one thing: ask

> Coaching is all about asking the **right questions.**

questions. Coaching is all about asking the **right questions**. It's amazing to know the power of "question probing." Coaches know what to ask, when to ask, how to ask, and who to ask great questions to take you from where you are now to where you want to be. A great coach asks great questions to help you remove the obstacles in your mind and to get you back on track in life and business.

A coach is someone skilled at unlocking your ideas with the right questions. A good coach knows that the answer to everything you need is within you. He or she helps you come up with the answer, instead of giving it to you. This leads you to think outside the box, clearing the petty and unnecessary stuff from your mind. A good coach focuses on the challenge and the possible solutions, enabling you to see the opportunity and options in front of you.

Effective coaching builds awareness and removes the excuses. Coaching will help you replace those excuses and limiting beliefs with empowering dreams, and boost your self-confidence. Coaching can help you identify your values, discover your "why," set goals, increase your self-esteem, and find a balance in life and business.

As importantly, here is what coaching is not:

- Coaching is not therapy—The process is about reaching success, not about fixing something that is broken, or in need of strengthening.
- Coaching is not mentoring—Coaching does not require close friendships.
- Coaching is not consulting—The answers are within you, not the coach. Their responsibility is to get it out of you.

- Coaching is not counseling—One does not negotiate with the coach about the process of accomplishment. A coach does not advise about the process, but instead, helps you discover the best path to success.
- Coaching is not problem-solving—The one being coached is responsible for taking action and resolving problems. They must own their circumstances and find solutions.

Coaching is the universal language to connect with people, helping them to develop a new perspective while expanding their inner beliefs and boundaries, as well as equipping them to become the best version of themselves.

Reflecting on my own experience, I had a coach—my father. Even though I was only twelve years old at the time, my father asked me questions to make me think. He didn't give me the answers. He cared enough not to impose his answers on me. He caused me to realize that I needed to come up with my own answers.

Having a coach is essential to your growth. Even if you commit to a "No Excuses" mindset, you can still be hindered by your lack of perspective. Even if you are asking yourself questions, you still may not have the clarity that you need for growth. This is where a coach comes in. Our awareness is limited by the fact that we only have one mind, one brain, one opinion—and a coach can solve many of these challenges.

Now one of the most commonly asked questions is, "How do I find the right coach?" Here are the characteristics you need to look for when choosing a coach for your life.

- Trust
- Clarity
- Experience

Identifying the Right Coach

Meet with your potential coach at least once before you commit to a coaching relationship. Take them out to lunch. Make sure they match to the following criteria:

- Chemistry Match: they have the ability to connect with you on a deeper level.
- Accountability: they are able to hold you accountable.
- Trustworthy: you need to be able to feel comfortable enough to share your concerns, challenges, and feelings with them.
- Coaching: they are able to bring out the best in you by asking the right questions at the right time.

It's important to remember that the coach doesn't need to be a professional. There is no formal coaching criteria; he or she simply needs to be wise. My father was my coach, and he never went to professional coach training. He just knew how to ask the right questions. In contrast, I have studied several professional coaching techniques, many of which simply reminded me of my dad asking the right questions and unlocking my mindset to find the solutions.

When you find someone with wisdom who has a passion and compassion to coach while meeting the above criteria, take action. They might be the one!

How to Coach

Coaching is essentially about growth. Even though there are many different coaching methods out there, their foundation is the same. As long as you have a coaching system you will be able to accomplish a successful coaching session.

I normally like to use the *GROWTH* model or *Integrity Coaching* model in my coaching sessions. Let's take a look at the GROWTH coaching process:

Goal—What is the particular objective that the prospective player is trying to achieve? More calls on clients? Better conversion from cold to warm contacts? How can I be of service to them in particular?

Reality—What is the current situation and what are the actual numbers we are measuring against? What circumstances are we attempting to overcome? Is there a clear understanding of what is at hand, and what is at stake?

Options—From this point forward, what alternatives does the player have to achieve their goal? Can the objective, or the goal, be reached by more than one method, and if so, how viable are each and which is the best alternative to pursue? What talents and skills do the player have currently in their arsenal, and which ones are best brought to bear?

Way forward—What is the action plan moving forward? How will you move the player from the current Reality towards the Goal, step by step with measurable success points in between?

Topic—Counter intuitively, a realization will develop that will allow the player to understand the underlying choices they make to target and attain success. They will reach a point in their life when the 'No Excuses' lifestyle will become their reality.

Healthiness—This is the conclusion of the process, where the player is debriefed, the entire coaching experience is reviewed, and the successes are identified.

If there is an area in your life—whether it's business, personal, or spiritual—that needs improvement, then you require the right coach to help you succeed. Coaching can help you identify your values, discover your "why," set GOALS, increase your self-esteem, and find the balance in life and business. Do whatever it may take to reach your goals. Coaching presents you with new perspectives that'll enable the necessary paradigm shift in order to live with a "No Excuses" mindset.

> "Unlocking a person's potential to maximize their own performance."
>
> – John Whitmore

Interact

The questions below will help identify potential coaches as well as help build the relationship you need with a coach, and consequently, with everyone else.

Vision: Am I stuck in a rut? Do I need a coach to help me expand my vision? Why?

Plan: Who can I bring into my life tomorrow that will encourage me to live with "No Excuses"? What connections am I making now that I need to take better advantage of?

Outcome: Are the people I'm surrounding myself with encouraging and uplifting me, or discouraging and bringing me down?

No Excuses Profile: Richard Mireles

Richard Mireles had a Vision. It wasn't in focus yet. But he did know how to motivate others already, and had discovered a mentor.

Richard wanted to go to college but had no knowledge of how colleges worked nor had the money to buy the necessary books. Now add a bigger obstacle: Richard was in prison.

His mentor, Mike, also a prisoner, made him an offer he couldn't refuse. Mike would give Richard a collection of books for a particular introductory class, but only if Richard pledged to do his best in school.

Mike went on to do something else a mentor does—he taught Richard about the book trade portion of college, wherein student trade the necessary books to other students, thereby saving a lot of money and making college even more affordable.

In 2005, he enrolled for some classes, and in three years, despite being behind bars, Richard accomplished something incredible. In the spring of 2009, Richard Mireles graduated with an Associates of Arts in Social and Behavioral Science. He never received less than an A. Richard has since gone on to complete a graduate program from Palo Verde College, with certificates as a Specialist with an internship program that will lead to a California Licensing Exam.

Richard's quote captures the "No Excuses" mindset perfectly.

"Someone once said, 'The sky is the limit.

'But how could the sky be the limit, when there are footprints on the moon?

'My life is no longer filled with excuses. It's filled with an *aim past the moon* perspective and that perspective has transformed my life. Today, I am a man who makes commitments, not excuses.'"

4. No Excuses—Personal Growth

The Importance of Growth

> "As human beings, our greatness lies not so much in being able to remake the world—that is the myth of the atomic age—as in being able to remake ourselves."
>
> —Mahatma Gandhi

It is a common adage that if a thing isn't growing, it's dying. Time's arrow only points from the past to the future; in all things, forward advancement is growth. Without forward progression, life is at its end. You can be good at something today, but if you are not growing with it, you will not remain good at it tomorrow.

Growth is only possible in an environment that is consistent, intentional, and positive. This is not an event; instead, growth happens daily, not in a day. Growth also takes purposeful action. You need to want it badly. You need to make it happen. You need to make it a habit. In order for growth to become a success, it needs to be positive. While you grow, you are also influencing people around you positively.

We are living in an era of constant evolution and development. It is a time of rapid transformations, inventions, and breakthroughs. If we desire to stay current, then our goals and goal-setting skills need to be revamped and become applicable to our time. The growth and transformation of technology are breaking through any past criteria or frontiers. The goals we set in this time need to be as boundless and seamless.

A great example of personal growth through the "No Excuses" mindset is Steve Jobs. When he set his goal to recreate the cell phone as we knew it, it was not the traditional type of goal with boundaries. His imagination fueled his goal. He dreamed bigger, better, and bolder. He did not restrain himself to a specific, measurable, achievable, realistic, and time-bound goal.

He had a vision and set it as his goal. Thanks to his courageous endeavor, we now have the iPhone. Therefore, now is the time to shift the paradigm. There needs to be a new platform with a new purpose for effective and modern goal-setting that will expand the potential, accomplish things beyond the imagination, and achieve extraordinary results. It is time to set **P.O.S.I.T.I.V.E. Goals™**.

P. Passionate: A P.O.S.I.T.I.V.E. goal is driven by passion. It fires you up and fuels your days with purpose, enthusiasm, and excitement. Your goal becomes pivotal to your daily exercises. It will create that burning desire within to bring your goal into reality. A goal that is fueled with passion will never burn out; it will only thrive.

O. Outside the box: A P.O.S.I.T.I.V.E. goal should not be bound by a criterion. It is not measured, limited, or simplified. Your goal pushes you out of your comfort zone and dares you to take risks. A P.O.S.I.T.I.V.E. goal gives you courage and enables your creativity. It will take you beyond the realm of expectation and imagination. Your goal is a manifestation of your wildest dreams; you wouldn't box up your dreams, right?

S. **Significant:** A P.O.S.I.T.I.V.E. goal enriches and benefits the lives of others, as well as add value to everyone and everything on its course. Your goal will create a win-win situation at any cost. The traces of significance that are left behind in the lives of others by your goal are as important as its fruition; for that too is its manifestation.

I. **Innovative:** A P.O.S.I.T.I.V.E. goal delineates between opportunities and challenges to creatively reach and surpass any hindrance en route its success. Your goal is constantly raising the bar and exponentially growing. An innovative goal is bigger, better, and bolder.

T. **Time-sensitive:** A P.O.S.I.T.I.V.E. goal requires a sense of urgency. This is key to achieving great results. Your goal will have a tremendous momentum that will fuel everything you do, because all things should work together towards its fruition. With a time-sensitive mindset you can hit and exceed your goals.

I. **Impactful:** A P.O.S.I.T.I.V.E. goal empowers, influences, and encourages. It is positive in intention, direction, and outcome. Your goal takes into account all the players of the game and all steps taken with purpose. With the right intentions, your goal will make an impact and a difference.

V. **Visionary:** A P.O.S.I.T.I.V.E. goal is multifaceted. Your goal belongs to a bigger whole. It is a piece of a larger impact. With a clear vision, your goal can identify and look beyond any limits or restrictions. It takes a visionary to recognize the true reality of their goal.

E. **Evolving:** A P.O.S.I.T.I.V.E. goal not only focuses on its final purpose but also in its process towards fruition. Your goal will help you develop new skills to achieve significant results. Setting a positive goal is embarking on a journey of transformation. As you shift the paradigm of goal-setting, you evolve yourself. The destination of your goal will be evolutionary.

> Setting a positive goal is embarking on a journey of transformation.

I would like to challenge you to plan your **P.O.S.I.T.I.V.E. Goals™**. Live your life with the passion and fire to achieve extraordinary results. Create an environment to grow consistently and to influence everyone around you positively. Your future doesn't have to equal your past. You are designed to achieve greatness, to be happy and to live the life you deserve. Start with setting a **P.O.S.I.T.I.V.E. Goal.™**

Personal Growth

Personal growth doesn't occur without effort. The effort is one of recognizing your own power, and taking ownership and responsibility for your own development. This approach, the "No Excuses" way of acting and deciding, means that one no longer expects others to make decisions for them, or that they no longer depend too heavily on others. It means taking charge of what you can change yourself.

Personal Growth: An Example in Action

Let's take a particular example and watch what happens when the intent to grow personally intersects an average life.

Paula is a typical modern mother. She has three children who are each involved in a different activity—soccer, ballet, and karate. They are all in school while she and her husband both work full-time jobs. These are incredibly busy people! In many cases, a mother like this would consider herself lucky to make it through the day.

She and her husband get the kids up and ready in the morning. She makes their lunches and drives them to school. She skids into work barely on time and works all day long while worrying about whether her children all made it to their after-school program.

Her husband works late, so as soon as she gets off work, she leaps into the car and races to taxi the kids to their various activities. By the time she's dropped them all off, it's almost time to pick them up again. She gets them home, gets their dinner ready right as her husband walks in the door, and by the time she's gotten them all to bed, she's so exhausted that she falls asleep on the couch without a moment to herself.

Paula's life was a constant exhausting blur, and she was fundamentally lost in it. Then, she heard about a different life, a different way of being; the 'no excuses' lifestyle. Suddenly, that other life wasn't going to be good enough for her anymore...

Paula wasn't content to remain in that life; she yearned for more. She made a decision to improve things, and that meant to improve herself. She invested some time in her personal growth. She did better at work and got a raise. She and her husband could then afford a babysitter who would pick up the kids after school and take them to their activities.

With that freed-up time, Paula was able to return home a little earlier. She learned that doing so meant that she had time to prepare dinner and still was able to have a little time to herself before her kids and husband came home. Already, she was seeing the benefit of no longer accepting or offering excuses. But the advantages didn't end there.

After dinner, she found that this change also meant she still had energy to spend time with her husband after the kids were asleep. To that time and energy, she dedicated intent to therefore improve her communication and relationship skill. And that little extra time is being used for further personal growth—it became a positive energy loop, freeing more time to improve things, to free up more time.

In only a few weeks, she took charge of more of her own time. Her advances included an understanding of delegation, to work with others to accomplish a common objective. Today, she is much happier, and gets even more accomplished than she did before. Like a set of dominoes, Paula's choice to invest in personal growth set off a chain reaction that affected almost every area of her life: career, finances, family, health—and this is only the beginning!

Personal Reflection

From my own story, of course there is a similar pattern—one that helped me define the "No Excuse" lifestyle more clearly than ever. In my case, when I started to grow, it impacted all aspects of my life in the same way. I discovered increased personal value, which when acted upon, increased my personal income, which then freed up more time to improve my personal value even more.

It is a cycle that repeats every time someone changes from a lifestyle that embraces excuses to the "No Excuses" mindset; their lives improve. When someone is growing, they have hope, faith, foresight, enthusiasm, passion, and fire. A growing person is thankful for what they do. Imagine how you would feel with all those traits yourself. That is what it is like to truly live with "No Excuses."

The Process

Achieving personal growth is not simple nor will it be quick. It's something that you have to work on each and every day, and it only happens when you have a system in place to help you. A lot of people give up on trying and expect growth to happen by chance. But it takes time, work, and commitment. Basketball superstar LeBron James understands the value of commitment, as noted in his quote:

> "Commitment is a big part of what I am and what I believe. How committed are you to winning? How committed are you to being a good friend? To being trustworthy? To being successful? How committed are you to being a good father, a good teammate, a good role model? There's that moment every

morning when you look in the mirror: Are you committed, or are you not?"

Successful people do what unsuccessful people aren't willing to do: work on personal growth. People want to upgrade everything—their house, their computer, their car—but they rarely think of upgrading themselves. Fulfillment doesn't come from top-of-the-line possessions and quantity of money; those things should just be considered a bonus. Fulfillment comes from developing yourself and being the best that you can be.

The rest of the world operates on a whole different level. Ninety-seven percent of people are doing the exact same thing that everyone else is doing; they are in the business of instant gratification. They do exactly what they have to do to get exactly what they want right away. Instant gratification, a stunt to your personal growth.

Nevertheless, personal growth is intoxicating. You want to grow, and as you grow you will find that you want to grow even more. It's a great feeling! There is a whole culture of people who are striving to improve themselves, and these are the people

> There is a whole culture of people who are striving to improve themselves, and these are the people who do what no one else will.

who do what no one else will. They allow themselves to be uncomfortable and they push themselves to grow each day.

You can bet that those people are leaving a legacy to influence and impact many other lives, and part of that legacy is "No Excuses." You should and can be a part of that legacy.

The right habits are critical.

Strive to be a part of that two to three percent. With "No Excuses," it's possible. See every challenge that comes your way as an amazing opportunity. It may not always feel that way and you may not like it, but it is true nonetheless. Every challenge that comes your way is an opportunity for you to do something remarkable. The "No Excuses" mindset is at its core the clear result of a "Personal Growth" habit. Personal growth will make all the other areas seem a bit less challenging, and it will put you one step closer to living with "No Excuses."

Abraham Lincoln and the "No Excuses" Mindset:

Probably the greatest example of persistence is that of Abraham Lincoln. If you want to learn about somebody who never quit, then look no further.

Lincoln was a champion and he never gave up. Here is a sketch of Lincoln's road to the White House:

- 1816 His family was forced out of their home. He had to work to support them.
- 1818 His mother died.
- 1831 Failed in business.
- 1832 Ran for state legislature—lost.
- 1832 Lost his job—wanted to go to law school but couldn't get in.
- 1833 Borrowed some money from a friend to begin a business, and by the end of the year, he was bankrupt. He spent the next 17 years of his life paying off this debt.

- 1834 Ran for state legislature again—won.
- 1835 Was engaged to be married but his sweetheart died leaving him with a broken heart.
- 1836 Had a total nervous breakdown and was in bed for six months.
- 1838 Sought to become speaker of the state legislature—defeated.
- 1840 Sought to become elector—defeated.
- 1843 Ran for Congress—lost.
- 1846 Ran for Congress again—this time he won—went to Washington and did a good job.
- 1848 Ran for re-election to Congress—lost.
- 1849 Sought the job of land officer in his home state—rejected.
- 1854 Ran for Senate of the United States—lost.
- 1856 Sought the Vice-Presidential nomination at his party's national convention—got less than 100 votes.
- 1858 Ran for U.S. Senate—again he lost.
- 1860 Elected president of the United States.

"Ever tried. Ever failed. No matter. Try Again.
Fail again. Fail better."

—Samuel Beckett

Fail Forward with the "NO EXCUSES" mindset!

Interact

You know the drill. Use these questions to raise your awareness to that level of developing personal growth.

Vision: What excuses am I using for delaying or ignoring my own personal growth? How do I see my own development over the next several years?

Plan: What steps do I need to take in order to improve myself? How do I need to rearrange my schedule to better serve my personal goals?

Outcome: In what ways could personal growth free up my time and make me more valuable to others?

5. No Excuses—Relationships

Why We Relate

> "Society is like a large piece of frozen water; and skating
> well is the great art of social life."
>
> —Letitia Elizabeth Landon

We humans are social beings. A great deal of our happiness, success, and experience in life rely on our interactions with other people. It is through our contact with others on a daily basis that we acquire knowledge, learn skills, develop our goals, and capture the chance at a better future. Meeting one person can unlock possibilities we never knew existed.

Unfortunately, in today's world, personal connections are becoming less and less common. We create excuses that stand between us and other people; excuses that separate us from the happiness and the prospects these people can present. In the previous chapters, we learned how a "No Excuses" mindset can help achieve our goals in different areas of life—but how can a "No Excuses" mindset in social relationships change our lives?

In order to better understand social relationship, we must understand their dynamics. There are three types of people out there; those who **lean**, those who **lift**, and those who **lead**. People who lean immobilize you; stay away from them.

People who lift inspire you; keep them near. People who lead positively influence you; seek them out.

I frequently go to Starbucks and find people standing in line waiting for their coffee. They are surrounded by others whom they could connect with, but instead of discovering these people, they are glued to their phones. Everyone is more focused on updating their Facebook profiles than on interacting with those around them.

As gripping as modern technology is, it has made it very easy for us to forget to connect with people. Even though technology is a blessing, it can also curse our society with ignorance of each other. We have become addicted to social media, and we let that addiction distract us from pursuing real relationships with real people. These technologies and 'social' outlets are excuses keeping us from getting out there, connecting with others, and seizing the opportunities that come with socialization.

In our fast-paced culture we have even found ways to take socialization out of social events! Instead of going to church or temple, many watch the services on television. People buy a seminar DVD or download and watch it instead of attending the seminar. These alternatives don't feed our human need to socialize, be part of the community, form relationships, and make friendships. Our dependence on technology causes us to miss on what is important leaving us unhappy and unfulfilled.

Returning to the line at Starbucks, I do the unexpected and unconventional. I high-five people, driving them to engage. Connecting with several people during these few minutes while waiting for my coffee makes both the connections and coffee more enjoyable. Not only is this rewarding to me on a personal level, it is essential to my growth professionally. That point has to be made indelibly. Engagement with people face to face is essential to personal and professional growth.

The Hidden Values of the Little Details

Whether or not you sell things for a living, building a solid relationship is an investment. You pay money, energy, and time to create and strengthen the relationship, and you get the values of social relationships in exchange. But the process is more than a one-for-one relationship, and both parties get more than they bargained for when they do what is necessary to maintain that relationship.

> Whether or not you sell things for a living, building a solid relationship is an investment.

Allow me to demonstrate this phenomenon. Last year I was a participant in an event and I met quite a few people, more than I usually do, that were of the same mind as myself on a lot of issues.

On the one hand, I received reminder emails and timely posts from the administrators of the event, reminding me of the upcoming dates, their special plans for this year, and so on. In the busy world in which we live, I had not even considered returning to the event, or rather, not on the basis of the one-to-one relationship I had with the administrators.

But on the other hand, I received a number of unsolicited emails from many of those like-minded people, in advance of the event. It was this group of people who took the time to make phone calls, to follow up, that made the most impression. It was their desire to keep the connections open, to remain connected, that convinced me to participate again.

In a world where the larger majority of society is careless, it's the small percentage of people who make the choice to be different and prioritize relationships that stand out. These people are not less busy than everybody else; in many cases, they are CEOs and executives. They simply made the choice to prevent being busy from becoming an excuse that hampers their social development.

Social media may be a great marketing tool but it is a personal connection that benefits a relationship. Mass emails are perfect for transmitting raw business data and information, but one-on-one contact is what really builds a professional relationship. Each of these things has its right time and place, and recognizing the difference is of utmost importance.

Often we forget that the little details matter the most. Take five to ten minutes a day to do the following:

- Daily act of kindness
- Writing a personal message or letter
- Showing gratitude
- Making a phone call versus a text message
- Adding value and significance to other's lives sincerely
- Personal, face-to-face visits
- Attending to the needy, nursing homes, hospitals, shelters, feeding the hungry, etc.

In order to ensure that you are getting the most out of the relationships you are building or improving, keep in mind the principles of the 3D mindset.

- Clarity of Purpose
- Plan of action
- The outcome

Mandating these principles even in your socialization practices will prove to be successful. Your purpose is to maintain, find and add value in your relationship, because healthy and valuable relationship bear fruit to successful individuals. Your plan of action is to make sure that you add that personal touch our world is currently devoid of. The outcome will be true, and will foster long-lasting relationships that are free from excuses but abundant in blessings.

> "I fear the day when technology overlaps our humanity.
> It will be then that the world will have permanent
> ensuing generations of idiots."
>
> —Unknown

Quality time and quantity time

The modern world is very different from the world of yesterday. In prior generations, workers sacrificed eight hours a day to enjoy their families and friends in the evening, and on weekends. Then as the demand for material goods rose, the cost of living rose as well, and suddenly, people are working overtime, working two jobs, or simply overworking just to keep up with their bills. Today, there are precious few people who can invest large blocks of time to endeavors, and even fewer who can pursue family relationships with what has become termed as *quantity time.*

The process of becoming the better person that the "No Excuses" lifestyle demands are going to require changes in paradigm, in the way you think of things and of time itself. Time is limited for everything, and one must realize how precious it is. Life demands that we take steps to prevent our hectic schedule from affecting our relationships.

To successfully operate at the levels that the lifestyle offers, one must learn to remain present in every activity. This new way of looking at life results from a realization that the only moment we can truly make a change is the one we are in RIGHT NOW. The world has terms for this distinction, and many will immediately recognize the difference. Having limitless time to do things, which is generally an impossible condition, is known as *quantity time.* Being present and fully dedicated to whatever focus at a given point is *quality time.* You may not be able to give quantity time, but you can definitely give quality time.

As a husband and father, I have interactions every day with my wife and children. Quantity time proponents would suggest I spend every moment possible acting in those family roles, offering to them my precious time. For that to be possible, I would have to forego the other obligations of life—work, community, and responsibility. It simply isn't feasible.

Let's say on the other hand that I only have three hours to dedicate to being a father and husband every day. Choosing to lock out all the other activities and dedicating these three hours wholly and purely for family, and nothing else, defines that time as *quality time*. For this new tenet to work, I must learn to be completely PRESENT for the duration without distractions or excuses.

If I am not thinking about work or business, and instead am fully immersed as a member, my presence engages my family members. We get together and create memories that live on forever. These memorable moments are of simple laughter, real communication, and fun challenges; they are about sharing your stories and your experiences. These are simple things that make QUALITY time, and these are the things that build and strengthen your relationship with your family. It gives us the intensity that brings us together.

Having daily Quality Time is a habit. We must open our hearts to love more. We must open our arms to hug more. We must open our eyes to see more, and finally, we must live our lives to serve more.

Developing strong interpersonal relationships by creating lasting connections instead of just passing acquaintances will take your business to a new level. In the same way, you should dedicate your time to build connections with your family and friendships to a "No Excuses" zone, a way of being that fully embraces the others.

Nothing can replace the human touch. Nothing can replace sitting and talking to another person, getting a phone call, or receiving a personal visit. This is why gathering around the dinner table every night is a cherished

> Developing strong interpersonal relationships by creating lasting connections instead of just passing acquaintances will take your business to a new level.

time you look forward to. It is the conversation with family and friends you crave, not the food. It is the experience of connecting with your loved ones, and because this experience is so precious, we have no excuses when it comes to relationships.

But the world's way, the convoluted and disoriented way, has built-in traps to confuse and confound us. Working toward the 'No Excuses' lifestyle offers ways to avoid these traps. At this point, let's look at these traps, and how we can learn to avoid them.

- **Relationship Trap 1: Social Media Is Enough**
  Technology gives us the ability to communicate to our families and friends in quick soundbytes and transfer of photographs through electronic means. Although modern technology has opened up so many possibilities to us, for business and personal life, it also represents one of the biggest traps possible that interferes with true communication and closeness. It is, in physical form, the difference between quality and quantity time because the constant output feels like we are connecting more, while in reality we are connected less.

  We falsely believe that emails, text messages, and social media can replace the personal touch we feel as we send out the messages, texts, and photos. But communication, true relationships, is a two-way process; texts, messages, and photos are all one-way broadcasts. Social media and texting are simply not enough.

Avoiding this trap is a matter of constantly making the extra effort to communicate directly and personally. Should I have the chance to meet the person or make a phone call, I will always choose the former. I will do that because texting and using social media cannot replace the value of the relationship; they are good things, but not good enough to keep my relationship alive. This dedication shows in the depth of my relationships. Sure, I do use the 'new media,' but I do so with sensitivity and intent.

Obviously, adapting to new forms of communication is essential, but it doesn't mean giving up the things that work, the things that give the most effect. We have to make the distinction between the situations that call for each method of communication. That is being responsible. That is discernment.

The intentional and widespread misuse of these new communication methods is a developing obstacle, a moving target that can interfere in the process of human communication. Choosing to accept no excuses, we can communicate far more effectively face to face, person to person. The telephone and telegraph before this offered their own challenges; overcoming the impersonal nature of the evolving business environment is dependent on our own responsibility to be the solution.

- **Relationship Trap 2: I'm Too Busy**
  "No one is busy in this world, it's all about priorities."

  —Unknown

The most pervasive mindset today is the one that says activity is equal to progress. That the more we are doing, the more successful we are. To a certain point it is true; the very process of moving toward a goal is in itself a success. But to a larger extent, all that extra effort is tantamount to pushing around deck chairs on the Titanic; it doesn't really do anything productive.

Many people fall into the trap of thinking they are too busy to take the actions that will lead them toward their goals. Some think they are too busy working to have good social relations. Others believe their relations and work prevent them from looking after their health. If you take a moment to examine those beliefs, you will see them for what they truly are: Excuses.

As every day has the same number of hours, the reality is that everybody is always busy. We only have a limited time in life, and even that person who manages to "have it all together" is still running as fast as he or she can. Nobody has an extra hour in their day.

So, the solution to this trap is a fundament of the 'No Excuse' lifestyle; focus your vision on the *why*. We need to always remember the reason we work so hard to advance. We do so to provide for our family and to have time for our friends. We should never forget the real reason that we're working, because it is that reason that overcomes the trap of being too busy.

- **Relationship Trap 3: I'm Not Needed**
  The third relationship trap is fundamentally a factor of our own self-assessment. It is a source of all kinds of excuses, and when we overcome this, we can accept our own self-worth, thereby disarming this category of traps altogether.

  When we reflect upon our relationships and do not see our value to others, it opens the floodgates of justifications for failure. For instance, if I believe that I am unnecessary, then the personal growth I would want would be a selfish waste of time and resources. EXCUSE. If I have nothing of value to offer, then I don't need to pursue interpersonal communication skills. EXCUSE. "My friends are all successful and they don't need me, so why bother trying?" EXCUSE.

  Self-doubt is as natural as breathing. So it isn't about having a feeling that we have to overcome, in order to defeat this trap. Instead, it is choosing to act in opposition to the feeling that overcomes it. Herein lies the key to virtually all of the "No Excuses" lifestyle. *It isn't about whether you feel your insignificance. It is about whether you take action to counteract that feeling.*

Having gone over the traps, let me put one more weapon in your arsenal through a story of my life; one that represents the importance of intentional relationships.

My father-in-law was overseas when he suffered from a stroke. The doctors called the family in the United States to inform them that he only had a short period of time to live, by their diagnosis. He had a large circle of friends and family who called him and sent him messages of support and good wishes.

Only two of his daughters decided to board a plane and fly for 24 hours to see their father. They dropped everything and went to see him, not thinking for a moment that he may not need them. No excuses kept them from acting and neither of them gave a single thought to the traps that could have kept them away.

To be fair, the diagnosis did not play out, and my father-in-law ended up living for another 9 years beyond the medical prognosis. The importance of this story is still pertinent today. The daughters had it right—nothing can replace the personal touch. Nothing can replace the love you show someone eye to eye. Nothing can replace the real value of a salesperson or agent. Nothing can replace a real human relationship.

Interact

Take these concepts to heart, and write your answers down in the space provided.

Vision: What value will I find and give in my day-to-day relationships with others?

Plan: How can I relate better to others? What steps can I take to invest in people's lives?

Outcome: What will my life look like when I invest in relationships?

No Excuses Profile: Roger Nielsen

Roger Nielsen's past is checkered with great success and low self-value, a high IQ, and a strong self-determination. He learned from the streets that there is more to a "No Excuse" mindset than just intelligence and knowledge. His challenge was not a lack of intelligence; it was a lack of self worth, self-confidence, and tenacity.

Shot three times and sentenced to prison at age 26 for a crime he was involved in when he was only 19 really shaped his life. In his own words: "I had a choice of making excuses or taking responsibility for my part in the crime. I chose to take responsibility, which led to my eleven-year prison sentence."

After leaving prison, he got a job and got involved in ministry. In that context he began to study after John Maxwell, a noted speaker and business leader. Since then, he has held jobs in many different fields and is in the process of developing his own education as well as becoming an associate trainer with EQUIP, John Maxwell's non-profit organization. He has traveled internationally to facilitate leadership roundtables with Fortune 500 companies and is even on the John Maxwell Team President's Advisory Council.

Management guru Peter Drucker said it this way, "There are two kinds of people in the world: those who make excuses and those who get results."

Roger Nielsen asks "Which one are you?"

6. No Excuses—Family

New Horizons, Same Challenges

"A happy family is but an earlier heaven."

—George Bernard Shaw

If anyone had excuses for not succeeding in America, I certainly did. When I came to the United States in 1998, I had $400 left in my pocket—and that was it! I wasn't in any position to get married; and even if I did, I wasn't anywhere near able to support the two of us on my income. I could have delayed marriage or family. If I had been looking for excuses to use, I could have found plenty: I did not know the culture or language, I did not own things that were considered the 'American lifestyle,' I did not have friends or family to help me get a job... the list of possible excuses went on and on.

I knew I would not fall prey to the excuses. I simply did what needed to be done. God blessed me with a wife who had faith in me because she saw how determined and single-minded I was in my desire to provide for her. I was going to do it! She too learned the language, the culture, and the business, and was very supportive of me. As I traveled, communication was and remains very important to us.

If I spent hundreds of hours building up my clientele in order to have a good income to provide for her, yet knew little of what she was doing, how she felt about an issue, or what was important to her, my hard work would have only given monetary rewards. But we both wanted more than that. We valued communication between us, and that in turn helped us reinforce our "No Excuses" mindset with each other. We did the right thing by looking at the challenges as opportunities for us to become strong individuals with a strong marriage and solid home. No excuses.

A "No Excuses" mindset in your family stems directly from your personal growth. If you are not growing as a person, the first impact will affect your family. You might control your anger, your tongue, or your sarcasm around employees or colleagues because of the possible negative repercussions on your livelihood. You might control your impatience, complaints, or moodiness around your friends because you don't want to lose their acceptance and the sense of belonging that being in their circle brings. But your family knows your shortcomings, and loves you anyway. So, because you are sure of their love and acceptance, you may feel like you can unload your burdens and be yourself.

When personal growth is missing, there is no peace. When you exercise little control over your thoughts and emotions at home, it gives license to other family members to adopt mindsets of complaining and negativity. Discontent, blame, and dysfunction show their ugly heads quickly and in surprising ways. The peace and growth of the family as a unit and of the individual members of the family are derailed because of the excuses that one person allowed to prevail!

A Place of Growth

When I was offered a job opportunity in Fresno, California, a quarter of the state from our home, I knew that I could not uproot my wife and young children from Los Angeles. I chose to forego what was easiest for me, and instead, was willing to do what was best for my family. My children knew that I was committed to that long commute every week and that I believed their security and stability were worth it. My family relied on me. No complaints. No long faces. No guilt tactics. No excuses. I chose their well-being over my own.

Thankfully, my wife had the same determination. She did not whine or complain about my absence. She knew we had to make that sacrifice for our children, and her strength and support never waned. The children responded to both of us with great appreciation and love. And they developed the "No Excuses" mindset as well!

This is an important lesson. When you decide to share the "No Excuse" lifestyle, or any other major life lesson, *modeling the desired condition directly is much more effective than preaching or lecturing—just do it!*

> *The home is your first school and where you learn life's most important lessons; families are the first teachers...*

It is in the home that the rough edges show and new areas of shortcomings surface; that gives more occasion for personal growth to take place in the home than in any other environment. The home is your first school and where you learn life's most important lessons; families are the first teachers of expected and acceptable mindset and behavior. Growth and new lessons continue throughout your life.

If you think that growth means perfection, let me assure you, it does not! You do not need to be perfect; instead, strive to be honest, admit to failures, learn to ask for and to give forgiveness, love and allow yourself to be loved. Accept and even celebrate differences in others; their "No Excuses" mindsets may look and function a bit differently than yours, but that is okay!

So now, let's begin to knit our concepts together, from earlier chapters. We are about halfway done, so it is a good time to link the ideas together and bring them all into a clearer view. We spoke early of developing a Crystal Clear Vision, to focus on the 'Why,' and let the 'How' take care of itself. We demonstrated how a focus on personal growth would impact all areas of life, and to this point we began to demonstrate how such changes affect us. We spoke of its impact on our own goals, how it influences friendships and other relationships. As this chapter turns to how it affects the family, perhaps you can begin to see the trend.

A "No Excuses" lifestyle will impact job, finances, relationships, spirituality, etc. Properly developed, it will elevate you in every area and facet of your being. The challenge is in the sobering reality that such a life change is permanent. You will be learning to overcome the challenges only to face them again and again. But the prize is worth the price, and the wonder of success is worth the work.

When you commit to personal growth and model how to turn obstacles into opportunities, your family will experience the value of learning and growing. They will follow your example, even if subconsciously. It will simply become part of your family culture and will be one of the most beneficial legacies that you can give them.

A Place of Success

We raise our children to expect to succeed in an environment where it is safe to talk about their fear and failures, trials and triumphs. They understand that we can fail but that we fail forward when something doesn't turn out like what they have envisioned. They must learn from it, change their perspective or method, and dive into it again. Giving up is not an option.

The truth is, the family is not just a place for challenges; it should also be a place of success. The "No Excuses" mindset is taught through modeling. The home is a place where we show our children that we can communicate, learn, and succeed together. The three favorite questions I have learned to ask my kids at least once a week are:

- What have you learned this week?
- What have you laughed about this week?
- What challenged you this week?

The younger we teach our kids to live with "No Excuses," the farther they can go in life.

A Place of Healing

Mother Teresa said, "The way you help heal the world is you start with your own family."

What needs to be healed in your home? What does your family need? What do you need? You need a place where you are understood and you understand. You need a safe place where you can be vulnerable, honest, and open, allowing others to be as well. You need a supportive and loving atmosphere where others share in your joys and sorrows, accomplishments and failures. You need to know that no one will harm you by words or deeds.

Be the kind of person who is a joy to be around. Caring for and loving others brings out the best in you and keeps your heart open to the unspoken and deeply buried needs of others. Because family and friends are the foundation of who you are, this is a realm where no excuses should exist. Give them your all without excuses.

Interact

This time, when you read and work through these questions, keep in mind the deep concept of family and how your actions affect those closest to you.

Vision: What are the characteristics I would like to see developed in my family? What are some traditions I want to begin with them?

Plan: What needs to change in my life to bring health and wholeness to my family? How can I model a "No Excuses" mindset for my spouse, children, and family?

Outcome: If I retain the status quo, where will it take my family? Will we grow closer together or further apart?

No Excuses Profile: Nick Vujicic

"Life without limbs? Or life without limits?"

Imagine being born without arms. No arms to wrap around someone, no hands to experience touch, or to hold another hand. What about being born without legs? Having no ability to dance, walk, run, or even stand on two feet? Now put both of those scenarios together, no arms and no legs. What would you do? How would that affect your everyday life?

Nick Vujicic, born in 1982 in Melbourne, Australia, without any medical explanation or warning, came into the world with neither arms nor legs. Imagine the shock his parents felt when they first saw him, their brand new baby boy missing arms and legs, especially as the pregnancy was uneventful and there were no family history to expect this condition. Imagine their dismay as they realized that the world would consider their firstborn imperfect and abnormal.

A limbless son was not what Dushka Vujicic, and her husband Pastor Borris Vujicic, had been expecting. How would their son live a normal happy life? What could he ever do or become when living with what the world would see as such a massive disability? Little did they know that this beautiful limbless baby would one day become someone who would inspire and motivate people from all walks of life, touching lives all over the world.

Nick Vujicic struggled physically and emotionally, as well as mentally when he was a child. However, with strong will-power, he finally came to terms with his disability. Nick said in one of his interviews: "I found the purpose of my existence, and also the purpose of my circumstance. There's a purpose for why you're in the fire." Nick wholeheartedly believes that there is a purpose in each of the struggles we each encounter in our lives and that our attitude towards those struggles, along with our faith and trust in the Lord, can be the keys to overcoming the challenges we face.

> "There's a purpose for why you're in the fire."

By using his own actions, Vujicic showed what it means to *never give up*. The news of his engagement must be yet another example of what it means to have a life that is truly without limits. Now he is happily married to Kanae Miyahara, and they have two beautiful and healthy children together. Amazing.

In 2010, Vujicic published the book *Life Without Limits*, in which he tells how he overcame his disability to live not just independently but to have a rich and fulfilling life, becoming a model for anyone seeking true happiness.

> "Attitude is everything and self-perception
> determines direction."
>
> – Nick Vujicic

7. No Excuses—Business

Pushing Past the Pain

> "Ninety-nine percent of all failures come from people
> who have a habit of making excuses."
>
> – George Washington Carver

A "No Excuses" mindset is crucial in the business world. Business is an unforgiving environment where opportunists feed on the unprepared and the sharks feed on those whose failures are attributed with excuses. For survival, entrepreneurs are constantly challenged to think outside the box. The globalization of many markets is continuing to create never-before seen obstacles and opportunities to the modern business person.

More than ever, 3D Thinking and a "No Excuses" mindset are the keys for success. Indeed, they have become of critical importance in the entrepreneur's toolbox. So how can we apply this concept to our careers?

I'll let you in on a little secret: the same approach I use at home is just as effective, and even more so, in the business world. As I have said, my family life is concentrated on quality time. In such an intense fashion, I personally spend 10 to 12 hours a day with my colleagues, employees, and team members. It's not that I'm a workaholic, I simply love what I do!

I live and breathe this conversation every day. It's what gets me up in the morning and energizes me throughout the day. The key principle is remembering that today and every day is a "No Excuses" day. It is going to be the best day. I make time for connections; I consider the other person's success as well as my own in every endeavor.

I put my whole self out there. I give it all I've got. I am present in every interaction. The key question is: What are you giving all of your energy to? Are you putting it into directed action toward your goal, or are you just spinning the wheels, trying to look busy?

7 I's of a "No Excuses" Business Mindset:

1. **Inspiration**: It's the source of energy to go beyond your ability.
2. **Incentive**: It's a multiplier of your willpower.
3. **Imagination**: It's what keeps the end result alive in your mind and leads you to overcome any excuse.
4. **Ideas**: Ideas are your major commodity; market and brand them well.
5. **Innovation**: The #1 indicator of being on the right track.
6. **Impact**: Shows your core values and solidifies your credibility.
7. **Influence**: Develops others to do more and to become more.

What electrifies you? What turns you on? What fires you up? What gets you out of bed? What's your WHY in business?

Find something you can walk towards and not away from.

Inspiration awakens our creativity, enables us to do the impossible, and improves our mental efficiency. It fires up the soul.

An uninspired mind creates a lack of energy for the body, resulting in a lack of performance filled with excuses. Surround yourself with everything and everyone that will help you feel your best, think your best, do your best, and be your best.

Interviews and Excuses

Over the years, I have had the opportunity to interview a lot of people from many walks of life. I offer them one of the best opportunities, the chance to become an entrepreneur. I offer them extensive training and support. A limitless opportunity dependent on their own actions and based on their potential.

Sometimes they have a real understanding of their objectives and are inspired to begin almost immediately to do business that will start them on their way to success. But more often than not, they are set in their own way with their own opinions. They are so focused on their immediate situation and what they feel that they often cannot envision the possibilities available to them. They are unaware that they could begin to correct their course today.

In nearly every case, the excuses begin with, "What you offer sounds good, BUT..."

And instead of giving rational explanations of how the program's mechanical flaws would prevent them success, they offer situational conditions instead, the very reasons WHY they should be pursuing my recommendations. Here are some examples, and I think you will immediately see why no excuse ever works.

"I have young children who require so much time and effort."

"My spouse and I only have one old and unreliable car between us."

"I just don't have the money necessary to make this system work."

As in every one of these examples, the kernel of knowledge that identifies the WHY someone should act is turned into an excuse why they won't. For the majority of cases, the issues people present for failing are actually the very reasons that they could achieve success if they put their minds to it. Amazingly, these people do not focus on the opportunities and the potential lying before them, but remain focused on their need.

The difference between poverty and prosperity is the mindset of living out of necessity instead of possibility.

There is a biblical passage that carries this to the ultimate conclusion, found in the 19th chapter of Matthew's Gospel. A certain rich man approached Jesus, proud of himself on one hand and fearful on the other. He outlines his wealth and his adherence to the Law, puffing himself up and patting himself on the back. But the next question he asks is very telling.

"What else must I do?"

Reflecting on what the man said, and obviously also what he knew of him, Jesus answered plainly, "Go and sell all you have, give it away, and come and follow me."

You probably guessed the outcome, if you didn't already recognize the story. The man went away discouraged, for he had many belongings. You see, the young man hadn't come to Christ for a simple answer. What he'd wanted was a validation of his excuse.

He had chased wealth, but had not found contentment. He had adhered to the Law, but had not found satisfaction. So he was hoping that Jesus would have a way for him to have the wealth and contentment. Jesus simply pointed out what his reason had been, and how shallow that reason was. Still, the excuse of gathering wealth was too powerful for the man to give it up.

> For as long as your why outweighs your excuses, you can accomplish anything.

The irony is almost laughable, were it not so pitiful. People dwell on the excuses that are holding them back instead of seeing them as the motivation to proceed beyond them.

You don't have enough friends? Go make some. Don't have enough money? Find ways to earn some. If you would put the same energy into doing what it takes to fix things, you would not be where you are right now! The excuse you try to believe is the reason you don't succeed.

What you choose to focus on most stridently, rather than a clear and concise solution, is your "WHY." For as long as your why outweighs your excuses, you can accomplish anything.

See how ridiculous it is to make an excuse in the first place? By turning your most strident excuse into your most passionate reason to succeed, you have changed your worldview, your paradigm. So now, even if you haven't yet fully committed to the lifestyle, you can more quickly focus your mind on the right question.

"What do I need to do to fulfill my *why* in the most efficient way possible? What must I do to overcome my excuses forever?"

You don't have to be the most educated or most experienced to start the journey, but the most willing to out-learn and out-work everyone around you.

Create Solutions

A "No Excuses" mindset does recognize the reality of your situation, but its emphasis is not on how to validate the condition—instead, it should be on how to solve the challenge the situation describes. How will you have the vision for a better career if you don't recognize your current state of discontent? How will you plan to develop new work habits if you don't see that the old ones are not working?

The difference is that instead of turning the reality of your situation into an excuse, a "No Excuses" mindset turns it into a purpose that will propel your career and your life beyond its current state. It shifts your perspective in every aspect of your life. The solution you seek to a situation is the very purpose for progress.

Imagine the challenges in your life—creditors, bills piling up, relational difficulties, health problems, etc. Each of these, by themselves, could be a sound excuse for failure. But turn that very point around and suddenly it is a "Why," a purpose to succeed. If it is simply "I need more money," then it should become "I need to find a better job," a reason for personal improvement, an idea that can be acted upon. Something upon which the "How?" will present itself.

Don't just do it once. Remember that every day is a "No Excuses" day. It is not enough to have the "No Excuses" mindset every once in awhile. You must get up every day and say, "Today I will only create solutions." This is the first step to developing new habits, good habits, the kind that lead to success. Good habits and intentional daily effort to turn excuses into solutions will help you become the person and entrepreneur that you want to be.

Invest in Yourself

You now have the means to define your objective. Your Crystal Clear vision should provide you a glimpse of the new universe, and should have turned your excuse for failure into purposes for progress. The shallowness of your previous failures has become a deep well of resources for success.

So now it is time to take the next step, the one we spoke of earlier. It is time for you to invest in yourself.

For the most part, we don't even know what an investment in ourselves would look like. We do know that investments are expected to yield a return. The idea that we can monetize our own value is an alien concept. But let me ask you, what would happen if you could see that return on investment immediately? Let's look at how such an investment might do just that.

As author and speaker Sidney Madwed put it, "If you want to be truly successful, invest in yourself to get the knowledge you need to find your unique factor. When you find it and focus on it and persevere, your success will blossom."

The key to *investing in yourself* is being able to see your potential, not just your actual value. Being able to visualize your value demonstrates that you are already picking up the skills of a 3D thinker. You have a vision of the kind of person you want to become. You have a plan to become that person through struggle and triumph. You understand the outcome of that investment. Believing and investing in yourself is the best way to shift your thinking from a paradigm of excuses to one of solutions.

Getting The Right Response

Making the transition to the "No Excuses" paradigm isn't instantaneous. Every issue we face leaves us with opportunities to find solutions or make excuses. So let's apply these principles of a "No Excuses" mindset to the sample excuses we demonstrated above. As professionals, we want to help people reconfigure their thinking, as well as overcome the objections that people present.

Remember those excuses we listed earlier?

"I have young children who require so much time and effort."

"My spouse and I only have one old and unreliable car between us."

"I just don't have the money necessary to make this system work."

Let's turn these excuses into whys.

"My kids are very young, and I want to provide for their fast-approaching future."

"My spouse and I share a car, but we can make early-morning carpools a special time."

"I don't have enough money now, but with a vision and a plan, I can grow what I have."

Do you see the difference? While the first group relayed a series of bad situations as if they were valid reasons for not pursuing their dreams, the second finds ways to shift their perspective and create new avenues of growth in their lives. Obviously, a person who takes on the second perspectives has a much better chance to succeed and immediately begins to attract success.

*You don't **achieve** success, you **attract** success.*

Which person do you think I will be more excited to bring on my team? The one who only looks to their current situation and makes excuses will be passed over time and again for promotions or new opportunities. The one who has a vision and creates solutions is the one worth investing in. It really depends on your willingness to look at things through the new lens of 3D Thinking and to change Excuses into Opportunities.

A Job Mindset vs. An Entrepreneur Mindset

JOB = Just Over Broke

It is very easy to get stuck in our current culture. We have been raised with the mindset of go to school, get a degree, find a job, and make a living. This unfortunately is no longer viable, especially with the fast-paced trajectory of our world. You can't just get by or make a living any more. You need more, and a job doesn't give you more. Entrepreneurship does.

While people with a job say,

I need to go to work tomorrow...

I will accept any job I can get.

I have to work more to make less than most.

I'm too busy to invest in myself.

Entrepreneurs say,

I love that life gives me choices. I choose to win, I choose to succeed, and I choose to live my dreams... I am an Entrepreneur.

I don't dream my dreams, I live my dream... I am an Entrepreneur.

I don't compete, I dominate the market... I am an Entrepreneur.

You are the most important person in your life. This is not to say you should be selfish, but when you neglect yourself, you are also neglecting people around you. The concept of personal advancement demands personal freedom to act. If your current environment feels like a trap, a burden, there are steps you can take to liberate yourself, one day at a time.

Discipline leads us to freedom, and freedom leads us to fulfillment.

Three simple ways to get Unstuck:

- Acceptance
- Decisiveness
- Change

Acceptance

The number one reason why people stay stuck is because they cannot accept that they are stuck. Accept that you are stuck, that something needs to change, that you have plateaued, and that you have stopped growing. Realize and understand who and where you are in life.

Be the hero of your own story. You were born to turn your mess into a message, and the test into a testimony.

Decisiveness

Indecisiveness is the number one reason for failure. Lack of ability to make a decision in a timely manner causes most people to fail with their projects and plans. Identify this challenge and decide to no longer let it be a setback from your success.

*"Decisiveness is a characteristic of high performing men
and women. Almost any decision is better
than no decision at all."*
—Brian Tracy

Change

Once you accept your circumstances and decide to take action, you can welcome change. Change is an opportunity to form new habits and become who you are meant to be.

Change is the process of conquering fear by getting out of your comfort zone and living daily in your God-given gift zone.

What happens if I follow my passion?

It is not important what other people are going to think. You have to decide every day to make the tough decisions. If you focus on other people's reactions to your decisions, rather than achieving your solution, you put your future and your success into the hands of people who do not have your interests at heart.

Instead, unleash your heart and mind from what *they* think. It may seem monumental, but at its core, it is simply giving yourself permission to take charge of your success by creating your own vision of your own future. From there, begin to build the 3D Mindset. Doing so will lead to a "No Excuses" mindset that recognizes that "what others think" is merely an excuse to stay in the past instead of taking the opportunities ahead of you.

Visualize, focus, decide, and act. If you follow these principles, you will find the career that suits your personality and ability. You will lead the life you've always wanted. So get out there and do something for your family, your friends, your colleagues and coworkers. Someday you will have your own story. Every time you overcome a difficult challenge you will have a story and that story is what changes lives.

So let's review what we have so far. In terms of achieving your own success, one must:

- Stop the excuses—convert them to purpose-driven solutions.
- Visualize your purpose and use the 3D Mindset to build your process.
- Invest in yourself to develop into the person you want to be.
- Strive to prevent new excuses from manifesting.
- Focus on the "Why," and the "How" will work itself out.

Successful entrepreneurs don't have better ideas; instead they have better *mindsets for taking action*. Action is what sets apart an aspiring entrepreneur from others. John Maxwell once said that "the biggest gap in the world is the gap between knowing and doing." Action means carrying out your plan to fruition, moving forward with projects, meeting and exceeding expectations.

ACTION requires ...

A -- **A**wareness, **A**ccountability, **A**ppreciation

C -- **C**ommitment, **C**lear conscience, **C**onfidence

T -- **T**rust, **T**enacity, **T**eamwork

I -- **I**nitiative, **I**nfluence, **I**mplementation

O -- **O**pportunity, **O**bedience, **O**pen mind

N -- **N**o nonsense, **N**oble purpose, **N**urturing nature

"Don't wait, the time will never be just right."

—Napoleon Hill

Don't wait for being completely ready for the plans and ideas you may have in mind. Take action now, and along the way you will learn and get ready. Most people would prefer to wait, wait, and wait until the perfect time has come for them to act. There is no such thing as the perfect time.

We live in the land of opportunities. People come from all over the world to hustle and work their way up to places that they could only imagine or dream of. But with this type of decisive and intentional action, any dream can become a reality and any purpose can be fulfilled. Find your noble purpose and defeat any residue of fear. Henry Ford once said, "You can't build a reputation on what you are going to do." You are either hot or cold; don't be lukewarm, because then you won't be of any value to yourself or others. Success requires action!

I would like to challenge you to decide to take action today on a dream, project, or idea that you have been procrastinating on for days, months, or even years. The joy that comes from the action is forever while the pain is only temporary.

There is a big difference between motion and action. Just because you get out of bed doesn't mean you are making progress. Taking action requires decisiveness, dedication, and clear direction.

Interact

Coming down to the wire here. So focus directly on your current situation, and discover the WHY that means the most to you.

Vision: What career opportunities am I missing out on by holding onto my excuses? Do I envision myself in the same place for the rest of my life?

Plan: How can I invest in myself today in order to prepare for the future? What steps can I take to "get unstuck" from my current situation?

Outcome: Am I content where I am? What would my career look like if I quit making excuses and start creating solutions?

No Excuses Profile: Jenny Marcos

Jenny Marcos had it rough. Born with Cystic Fibrosis, a genetic disorder that affects the lungs, leading to chronic illness and early death, hers is a posthumous profile in courage and determination.

In 2011, her condition reached catastrophic levels. Despite having to battle many lung infections and endure much hospitalization, she was courageously building her own insurance business. She always had a serious passion to excel. I was proud to personally assist her in developing the 3D Mindset that helped her remain on a "No Excuses" trajectory.

In one year she achieved every accolade that was available, sales records, plaques, and contests. Furthermore, she was promoted to mentorship within 6 months. Her physical conditions had deteriorated to the point where she was in need of a lung transplant in order to stay alive.

Listen to her testimony in her own words:

"I exercised every day, even with the very little lung capacity I had. Regardless of how I felt, I did not cave in. I had a schedule and I had daily goals. No excuses meant no excuses. I did what I had to do to make sure I stuck to my regime.

"I practiced meditation and prayer every day. I am a humbled student of the universal laws, so much so that I only allowed thoughts, words, and actions in harmony with those laws. I ensured my practice of positive thoughts, words, and actions. I only allowed others to speak and act positively around me.

"Within 3 weeks, I managed to walk out of my hospital room on my own and I did not have to resort to life support. My breathing tests were the best I had ever achieved in 2 years since lung transplant approval, and the doctors and medical staff at the hospital were astounded by my progress.

"To this day, they cannot believe my progress, and even though I am not cured of my illness, the power of my mind and my "No Excuses" mindset is what drives my life. My circumstances, other people, or any negative thought or force can't stand in the way of my goals and dreams.

> My circumstances, other people, or any negative thought or force can't stand in the way of my goals and dreams.

"My story has impacted so many lives since my life has transformed. I have told it so many times that it inspired me to write a book about my life and my transformation. I have changed so many people's lives for the better. This encouraged me to become a life coach, following in the footsteps of my mentor, Mr. Farshad Asl, in personal and business development.

"I live by the "no excuses mindset" and I would put my integrity on the line for what I have learned firsthand from Farshad. My mentor and friend in life and in business."

Unfortunately, Jenny Marcos passed away in August of 2015. She fought the good fight, and never surrendered her mind. I am sure there are so many Jennys out there fighting against health issues that they have no control over, but with the right mindset, they are making a difference in their communities and without excuses.

Now, how can you allow yourself any excuses?

8. No Excuses—Legacy

> "Carve your name on hearts, not tombstones. A legacy is etched into the minds of others and the stories they share about you."
>
> —Shannon L. Alder

LEGACY (noun)

- Something old or left behind
- Something of monetary value
- Money or property left to someone in a will
- Inheritance from a will
- Outdated or discontinued

What comes to mind when you think about the legacy you want to leave behind? Will it be relatable to the definitions above—something of monetary value, an inheritance, the totality of who you are left behind in a will? Or is there a deeper resonance? Does a legacy mean more to you than a will and some inheritance?

LEGACY is a word I hold close to my heart. It is part of my being and pertains to my leadership and developmental growth. It goes beyond any materialistic memorial of who I am. It runs deep. A legacy is the impact and impression an individual makes and leaves behind in the lives of others; it no longer represents the individual, it represents the people who carry on his or her name with passion and integrity.

Transformational Process of Living and Leaving a Legacy

Transformation takes place within us when we learn to be intentional and go from focusing on... to...

- Me ... to... others
- Success ... to ... significance
- Limited ... to ... limitless
- Scarcity ... to ... abundance

The indicators of this process are:

- When you utilize the 3D Mindset to turn your excuses into impact.
- When you utilize the 20/20 Mindset to go from victim mentality to victor mentality.
- When you utilize the Paradigm Shift to turn your problems into opportunities.
- When you utilize the "No Excuses" mindset to go from making a living to making a difference.

When you are no longer preoccupied with focusing on *me* and instead focusing on others, a legacy becomes the significant outcome.

Facing the Cancer

> "The things you do for yourself are gone when you are gone, but the things you do for others remain as your legacy."
>
> —Kalu Ndukwe Kalu

According to the American Cancer Society in 2016, there will be an estimated 1,685,210 new cancer cases diagnosed and 595,690 cancer deaths in the US.

It was a couple of days before Christmas and I was driving to one of my offices when I received a call from my doctor insisting I see her right away. A couple weeks prior, I had a very small bump removed from my thigh as part of a routine check-up. I'd had this small growth for some time and didn't think anything of it.

Despite the doctor's insistence, my reaction was to put her off and not take her request seriously. I was focused on getting to the office and reminded her that I was very busy, going so far as to suggest seeing her next year. Nevertheless, through my wife's persistence and encouragement, I drove to the doctor's office.

I was told that the small bump I'd ignored for so long was cancerous and could have possibly spread throughout my body. To make matters worse, I couldn't see an oncologist until after the holidays and the New Year. I felt like everything had come to a complete stop and I was sitting in a void without sound or feeling. This was the first time I'd heard of anyone in my family having cancer, let alone knew where to begin or how to deal with the news.

Saying I was overwhelmed with the situation was an understatement. All I could do was worry and reflect on life. I wondered if I had told my wife and daughters how much I loved them often enough? Had I told my team members at work how much they meant to me and that I valued working with them?

I also realized that a tremendous shift was occurring within me. I began to realize that I'd been too busy to think about my life. My entire focus had been on my business. Now the paradigm was shifting and new perspectives were unfolding.

I felt God wanted me to reflect for the two weeks before I found an oncologist. This experience was much more than fighting cancer, it was an important life-changing opportunity.

What once seemed important didn't matter anymore. Previously, being busy at work had changed to being efficient. Communication had transitioned to connecting with people. I realized that striving for quality time and not quantity was the best time spent with my family.

It became crystal clear to me that it wasn't about spending time with people; it was about investing time with people and creating memories with them. I was taking a stern look at how I had placed a lot of value on success. That too had changed with my need to live a life of significance.

> It became crystal clear to me that it wasn't about spending time with people; it was about investing time with people and creating memories with them.

I've learned to think of challenges not as being bad or a setback, but as an opportunity to grow and take action. For some, a challenge is a roadblock and an easy way to give up. They can become easy excuses. Challenges are part of our everyday life, some greater than others.

When I heard that dreaded word *cancer*, and found out I would be fighting for my life, several questions came to mind, three of them crucial to my current challenge. These questions became critical to my transformational journey.

My 3 questions were:

1. Do I live my life to the fullest?

2. Do I tell the people around me (family, friends, my team) that I love them and I care about them?

3. Do I live a life of significance?

My answer to these questions were "NO" at the time.

These questions were foundational to switching from an expressed desire to live, to actually living the life that I have today. A true paradigm shift took motion. It gave me the clarity in mind (20/20) that I needed to change the direction of my life. It provided me with the 3D Mindset, and finally, a life with "No Excuses" mindset.

I am grateful that cancer, as scary as it was, triggered this transformation in my life. My challenge became a blessing in my life. I learned that God has given each of us a *reason to live*, *a purpose*, and *a greatness* to serve others.

When the time came for the truth to be revealed about my cancer, I didn't know which to be more excited about, my transformation or my second chance to live. I had the cancer removed and learned it had not spread throughout my body. I was cancer-free!

After a few months, I was given the opportunity to travel to Guatemala and serve with 150 other John Maxwell coaches and speakers. We trained 19,000 leaders during the week we were there. The transformation that grew within me became so much more significant once I was serving others. Soon, this transformation began to make its impact on the lives of the people in Guatemala.

I started to build better quality relationships with my family, my friends, and my team. My business grew as a result, like never before. We built one of the largest organizations in our company. My kids hear daily about how much I love them. My team knows how important they are to me. I am here to serve them, coach them, and partner up with them to become what God wants us to become. We will achieve our fullest potential in life and business.

I can't help but rejoice in this triumphant transformation. I have become liberated from excuses and freed from boundaries. I am happy to proclaim that I now answer those three questions with a "YES." As long as I live an intentional life, I can continue serving and growing with others while adding value to the world.

Through this transformation, my mission became refined, my legacy crystallized. My mission in life is to *develop leaders who inspire leadership in others, leaving a legacy of impacting the lives of people we touch with passion and integrity.*

No Excuses LEGACY = LEADERSHIP + LOVE

Leadership:

A long lasting legacy requires both servant leadership and unconditional love.

Let us begin with Leadership.

Leaders are defined by the following characteristics found in Legacy.

Leadership

Enthusiasm

Generosity

Authenticity

Compassion

Youthfulness

- **Leadership**—John Maxwell said, "Everything rises and falls on Leadership."

Often, the perception is that to be a leader you need to be older and more experienced; being something that occurs towards the end of your life. Not true. LEGACY plays an important role in defining a good leader at any age. Leadership is not only about producing results or measuring success with statistics. Leadership is doing something with significance that makes families, organizations, societies, nations, and the world a better place before you die.

Leadership is the act of serving others and has no gender or age preference.

- **Enthusiasm**—People who intensely believe in their purpose leave a legacy behind.

It's the difference of being laser-focused on what can be done instead of allowing inertia to set in. Enthusiastic people take action rather than setting up roadblocks or distractions. What helps grow enthusiasm and build on the momentum is to have a clear vision of what motivates you to remain focused.

- **Generosity**—Generosity is a strength, not a weakness.

Generous leaders are servant leaders. They always come with open hands and an open heart. Generous leaders have faith in others to succeed. In turn, they receive tenfold loyalty, commitment, and a positive outcome.

- **Authenticity**—It's not what you tell people but how you make them feel.

Authentic Leaders are not afraid to show emotion and vulnerability as they share in the challenges with their team. Developing a solid foundation of trust with open and honest communication is critical to authentic leadership.

- **Compassion**—The secret to long-term relationships is providing kindness, care, and love.

A leader's purpose is to provide knowledge and generate trust through kindness. This will provide a foundation that allows others to make choices, right or wrong, and grow in a positive manner from the experience. Taking the time to go the extra mile when needed is the best way to develop solid leadership. Compassion is that special

> Compassion is that special ingredient that is often missed, and it makes a difference in building a positive environment.

ingredient that is often missed, and it makes a difference in building a positive environment.

- **Youthfulness**—We often think that leadership is something that only occurs when you're older.

Successful leaders leave a legacy behind at any age. The "Y" in legacy is to remind us that our future leaders are young and energetic, full of new ideas. The "Y" can be for generation Y. Mellenials are eager to embrace the vision and principles of Leadership head on. Based on research done by Virtuali, a leadership training firm and consultancy, and Workplace-Trends.com, "The Millennial Leadership Study" revealed that out of 412 millennials, 91% of millennials aspire to be a leader and out of that, 52% were women. Nearly half of the millennials defined leadership as *"empowering others to succeed."*

Love:

Legacy requires love just as much as leadership. Now, Love isn't only about romance and marriage; it is much more than that. It plays a fundamental role in every aspect of our lives, personal and professional. **Love elevates the beauty of life**, and just as importantly, it also impacts your business, leadership, and influence. You can't lead without love, and more importantly, you can't leave a legacy without love.

To better illuminate this concept, we must understand the power and potential of love. **Love is the force behind success** in all aspects of life. Fear is what holds everyone back from achieving their dreams and attaining success. Often it is thought that courage is the opposite of fear. Nevertheless, this is not true. Love is the opposite of fear.

FEAR is **F**alse **E**vidence **A**ppearing **R**eal

While,

LOVE is **L**eadership through **O**ptimism, **V**alues, and **E**ndurance

> "There is no fear in love. But perfect love drives out fear,
> because fear has to do with punishment. The one who
> fears is not made perfect in love."

> —1 John 4: 18

When your leadership and legacy is built on love, obstacles are overcome through love's fruit of optimism; foundations are built solid and secure in love's values; and success is achieved through the strength found in love's endurance. True leadership and success in both personal and professional life are derived from love.

> "Dear children, let us not love with words or speech but
> with actions and in truth."

> —1 John 3: 18

Journal your daily experiences

Through my transformation, I gained a very valuable and practical habit. I began to journal daily about:

- Experiences
- Lessons learned from them
- Feelings felt from them

I often found myself with great ideas and emotions throughout the day and discovered that journaling every night would help me retain them. I had found a tremendous value of journaling nightly. Every morning I would start with a clean slate, without worries of forgetting yesterday's values. The journal not only became my outlet, it became my written record of both accomplishment and trial, of results and consequences.

My journey is by no means complete, but I have already learned some very valuable lessons along the way. One of the things I have learned has actually become my new motto: "Life By Design, Not By Default!" Though this is the first time I have addressed it in this book, this very simple statement is an affirmation of the central theme of the "No Excuses" mindset. Living by intent a life that leaves behind a respected and valuable legacy is so much more than just feeling better about one's self, or chasing more stridently a personal goal of success.

Everyone leaves behind a legacy of some kind, but those who approach living with a 'No Excuses' mindset leave a legacy of value. A life hidden behind the veil of excuses leaves behind a blank page, but a life with the brilliant light of purpose shone upon it fills every page with wisdom.

"Life by Design, not by Default" means we change before we have to. It is a life of intentionality. It is a life of discipline. It is a life of focused priorities. If you're still breathing, you have the power to lead your life.

Living in thanksgiving daily is a habit. We must open our hearts to love more, we must open our arms to hug more, we must open our eyes to see more, and finally we must live our lives to serve more.

Interact

Let's close this book, the same as the other chapters, with questions.

Vision: Did I live life to the fullest today? Did I live the way I wanted to live, meeting my ideals?

Plan: How can I love the people around me? How can I leave something worthwhile behind? If I should pass away unexpectedly, can I leave this life with no regrets? Am I ready to go?

Outcome: What would happen if I lived a life of significance? If I had a little more time, what would I change?

CONCLUSION: Are you ready to build your legacy, a legacy of which you and your family can be proud?

Epilogue: "Am I Going To Make It?

> "Entrepreneurship is living a few years of your life like most people won't, so that you can spend the rest of your life living like most people can't."
>
> —Anonymous

"Am I going to make it?"

This is a question we all ask at least once in our lives. We all have goals and aspirations we hope to achieve, but the question should be rephrased.

"What do I need to do to make it?"

As an entrepreneur, I, along with many others, face this question on a regular basis. In order to alleviate these doubting thoughts, I've lived and developed a foolproof criterion that assures success. If you meet all five points, then I can undoubtedly assure yourself that YES, you will make it!

Dream

First and foremost, do you have a dream? Your dream will be the destination of your entrepreneurship. Is your dream crystal clear? A crystal clear dream shows you exactly where you want to be. This kind of dream is uncontainable. You simply can't wait to share this dream with others. The excitement is contagious, resulting in others wanting to be a part of your dream. Sharing your dream creates for you a sense of purpose and direction as you leverage the added excitement into building a successful team and business along the way.

Purpose

Do you have a purpose? If your dream is filled with purpose, you are one step closer to its mani- festation. Purpose is the fuel that propels you toward your dream's

> Purpose is the fuel that propels you toward your dream's destination.

destination. It is crucial to understand that your dream is the destination but purpose is fuel for all of life. A purpose- driven life is a productive one.

The next step is to focus on the WHY. Understanding the importance of your purpose helps your mind develop the HOW. For example, what do you want to fulfill with your purpose? What impact do you want to make? What transfor- mations will you ignite? What is it about your purpose that presses you forward, moves you toward success?

Once you have identified the key characteristics of your pur- pose, the choices to act upon will become evident and your purpose will become a solid foundation for your dream.

Passion

Do you live your life with passion? A successful life integrates passion into one's work and personal life. The passion in your life is the fire that lights and warms your way toward your purpose-filled dream. Nothing significant has ever taken place without passion. As an entrepreneur, I must love everything I do; otherwise, I have set myself on the opposite trajectory from success. With love and passion, anything can become attainable, bearable, and possible. If you push your heart into your work and dreams, you will succeed.

A life filled with passionately pursued purpose and dreams is filled with value. Not only do you gain and build value into your business, you infuse your dream with added value in the lives of others. This is the power of passionate, driven dreams.

Putting gold through fire makes it purer, brighter, and more beautiful. Treat your work, goals, dreams, and yourself as gold; put yourself through the fires of passion and bear witness to remarkable results.

Ability

Do you have what it takes to bring your dream to fruition? Is it in your power and capability to take on the tasks at hand to make your dream a reality?

Here is the moment of truth. You must be honest and candidly self-reflective. Being reasonable and realistic is key. Your abilities are the tools you need to reach your destination. IF you are not built for a specific cause, then it becomes futile to reach for something not meant for you.

For example, I sing loudly, if not well. My daughters constantly taunt me humorously, asking that I not sing with such fervor. I am not designed to be a singer. No matter how hard I try, or whatever time I spend in practice, my voice simply will never be 'excellent.' Working however diligently, with all my best efforts and intent, I could only become at best an average singer.

Instead, I believe one should develop one's strengths. If you're already equipped with certain abilities and gifts, then invest in those. When in pursuit of success, realize your gifts and identify your skills and abilities. Act on them, and with the right engine of a passionate, purposeful dream, you can reach the top.

Attitude

Last, but far from least, do you have the right attitude for success? I am always emphasizing that you need to work more on yourself than on your job. This increases the value you put on yourself, and thereby affect the value that others are willing to put on you. The best way to improve your own worth is by enhancing your attitude. When on the road to success, your attitude will determine the speed at which you travel toward your dream. With the proper mentality, you make better choices, make the right impacts, meet the right people, and gain the unseen advantages that spawn from other people wanting to work with you. You are your own greatest challenge. If you overcome your own weaknesses with the right attitude, then success becomes a given outcome.

If you see yourself manifesting these five points, then I would like to say,

"Congratulations!"

If you have a dream, a purpose, passion, the ability, and the right attitude, then you are set for success. If you find you have a weakness among these, then you can focus on it and bring it to bear fruit in your life. Stop looking for excuses and start doing what it takes to realize your dreams.

Notes

Abraham Lincoln. (n.d.). Retrieved 2015, from The History Place: thehistoryplace.com

Allen, J. (2014). *As A Man Thinketh.*

Benedict, E. L. *Brainology: The Mindset of Successful People.*

Curtis, D., & Anthony, R. (n.d.). *Introduction To Peterism.* Retrieved April 2016, from ecclesia.org

Downey, M. (2008). *The TGROW Coaching Model.* Retrieved 2016, from Personal Coaching Information : personal-coaching-information.com

Maxwell, J. C. (2012). *15 Invaluable Laws of Growth .*

Maxwell, J. C. (2012). *21 Laws Of Leadership.*

Maxwell, J. C. (2015). *Intentional Living.*

Vujicic, N. (n.d.). Retrieved 2015, from Life Without Limbs: lifewithoutlimbs.org

FARSHAD ASL
LIVE WITH PASSION

For a Life-Changing Experience

Invite Farshad Asl to speak at your next event.

Author, Entrepreneur, Leadership Coach, International Speaker, & Regional Director of Sales for Bankers Life

ARE YOU READY TO EXCHANGE EXCUSES FOR EXCELLENCE? Does your business, organization, or community need a new mindset? Are you overdue for a paradigm shift? Are you ready to learn an innovative way to overcome life's challenges? If so, then Farshad Asl will exceed your expectations. It's time you became the person you are destined to be.

Live a life of passion, purpose and clarity with "No Excuses."

Reach Farshad Asl at:

TopLeadersInc.com

FARSHAD ASL

LIVE WITH PASSION

Live a life of passion, purpose and clarity with *"No Excuses."*

"There are life stories and then there are stories that change lives. *The "No Excuses" Mindset* is filled with real life stories that will change your life. This will be a book you will want to use as a guide as you live out your own life story."

—Paul Martinelli, President The John Maxwell Team

"Farshad is a leader who sets high standards for himself as a leader and that is the secret to his success. In *The "No Excuses" Mindset* he shares with us the ways we can take decisive actions, providing us with a new landscape of opportunity in how we live our lives and lead our business."

—Deb Ingino, CEO Strength Leader Development

"With compelling candor and masterful storytelling, Farshad Asl serves us rich content forged from his proven process. *The "No Excuses" Mindset* opened me up to what's possible personally and professionally."

—Kary Oberbrunner, Author of Day Job to Dream Job, The Deeper Path, Your Secret Name, and ELIXIR Project

"Everyone should read this excellent book to develop a *"No Excuses"* mindset. You'll be inspired by Farshad's life story and others who are testaments to applying a 3D Mindset. These practical ideas will dramatically impact your business, professional success, personal life and family."

—Mike Esterday, CEO, Integrity Solutions

"*The "No Excuses" Mindset* is a book about purpose, passion and perseverance. It explains the journey of every successful person who dared to follow their dream. Farshad not only shows you his journey to achieving his dream; he has created a roadmap to enable you to achieve yours!"

—Johnny Walker, MA, CPC, Founder, Foundational Core Values™

"This book is a gift to anyone who reads it. Farshad Asl lives this message, making this book an inspirational and practical handbook for eliminating the excuses that would hold you back. In fact, as you read these pages you will not only be stripped from the excuses you've relied on but some new ones will be revealed. I dare you to begin at once!"

—Scott M. Fay, Vice President, The John Maxwell Team

Reach Farshad Asl at:

TopLeadersInc.com

CPSIA information can be obtained
at www.ICGtesting.com
Printed in the USA
LVHW01*1229070618
579911LV00002B/2/P